Imye kuchazev

NINA GOURFINKEL

Translated by Ann Feshbach

Gorky

Evergreen Profile Book 17

GROVE PRESS, INC.
NEW YORK

EVERGREEN BOOKS LTD.
LONDON

Library of Congress Catalog Card Number: 60-7387

Evergreen Profile Books are published

in the United States by Grove Press, Inc.

64 University Place *New York 3, N.Y.*

in Great Britain by Evergreen Books Ltd.

20 New Bond Street *London, W. 1*

Distributed in Canada by McClelland & Stewart Ltd., 25 Hollinger Rd., Toronto 16

First published in France by Editions du Seuil, Paris, as Gorki par lui-même

MANUFACTURED BY MOUTON & CO., IN THE NETHERLANDS

Gorky
by Nina Gourfinkel

Contents

Фома Гордѣевъ

X

— Любаша! — сказалъ однажды Маякинъ, придя домой съ биржи. Сегодня вечеромъ приготовься — жениха привезу! Закусочку намъ устрой посолиднѣе... Серебра стараго побольше выставь на столъ. Вазы для фруктовъ тоже вынь!.. Что-бы въ носъ ему бросился нашъ столъ! Пускай видитъ, что у насъ что ни вещь — рѣдкость!

Любовь сидѣла у окна штопала носки отца и голова ея была низко опущена къ работѣ.

— Зачѣмъ все это, папаша? — съ неудовольствіемъ и обидой спросила она.

— А для соуса... для вкуса... И для порядка. Потому — дѣвка не лошадь, безъ сбруи съ рукъ не сбудешь.

Любовь нервно вскинула голову и бросила прочь отъ себя работу, вся красная отъ обиды взглянула на отца... и снова взявъ въ руки носки, еще ниже опустила надъ ними голову. Старикъ расхаживалъ по комнатѣ, озабоченно подергивая рукой свою огненную бородку, и глаза его смотрѣли куда-то далеко и было видно, что весь онъ погрузился въ какую-то большую и сложную думу. Дѣвушка поняла, что онъ не будетъ слушать ее и не захочетъ понять, какъ унизительны для нея его слова. Ея романическія мечты о мужѣ-другѣ, образованномъ человѣкѣ, который читалъ-бы вмѣстѣ съ нею умныя книжки и помогъ бы ей разобраться въ смутныхъ желаніяхъ ея — были задушены въ ней непреклоннымъ рѣшеніемъ отца выдать ее за Смолина; были убиты, разложились и осѣли въ душѣ ея горькимъ осадкомъ. Она привыкла смотрѣть на себя, какъ на что-то лучшее и высшее обыкновенной дѣвушки купеческаго сословія, дѣвушки пустой и глупой, которая думаетъ только о нарядахъ и выходитъ за мужъ почти всегда

Man is the sole marvel on earth, everything else is the product of his intelligence, his imagination, his creative will. If he has invented gods, it is because he did not succeed in materializing all the good he carried within him.

GORKY

A NEW LITERARY HERO

Gorky, the Bitter. In choosing this pseudonym, Alexei Maximovitch Peshkov revealed the key to the characters he was to describe. No doubt the choice of his pen name was inspired by the epithet which always accompanies the word "destiny" in popular Russian sayings – "bitter destiny." Such was the destiny of the new heroes he was to introduce into literature.

Gorky came on the scene during the last ten years of the nineteenth century, at a time when social as well as literary canons were being upset. Although his first writings brought only superficial innovations to both of these areas, the thirst for novelty was such that they soon won the attention of the Russian public and the world.

At the turn of the century, Russian literature was glutted with poor imitations of the realism that Tolstoy, Dostoevsky, Turgenev and Goncharov had brought to perfection. But their books, still quite recent, no longer satisfied the reader. Their world, the world of the declining nobility, had come full circle. Their problems were no longer moving. The public strained towards the future, a revolutionary future. Dostoevsky continued to influence thinking through the universal value of what he wrote. But this man, whose revolutionary association had sent him to prison, returned a loyal subject, obedient to the monarchy and orthodox in religion; his novel, *The Possessed,* was a biting caricature of the revolutionaries.

The second-rank writers, populist-inspired – Korolenko, Verassaiev, Gleb Uspenski, Pomialovski, Grigorovitch – stood out from a crowd of minor naturalists, taking as their subject the drabness of daily life. Repeatedly, they returned to the themes of the suffering of the people, their oppression, their apathy. Chekhov, the truly great writer of the time, did so more than the others; like the others, he held out no hope; through his work ran the drama of social as well as literary renunciation. Last realist of the long line, through his very excessive exactitude, through his precision and his purity of detail, as Gorky put it, he "kills realism."

Of course, there were several attempts at a Symbolist revival, but, burdened with "decadence," they were viewed as foreign importations and cast aside as poetry. Symbolism had its magnificent comeback at the beginning of this century with the arrival of Alexander Blok; it found, however, only a limited audience. For among the major layers of the public, the realist tradition was too deeply rooted, too closely linked to the socialist ideal of the closing century, for "art for art's sake" to be taken seriously. In poetry as well, the few fine poets remained unknown, but the "citizen poets" with their theme of "universal suffering" were carried to the heights. Paradoxically, Nekrasov, the creator of new rhythms and novel poetic images in which he blended folksong with his polemic, was esteemed for "his ideas" only, and "pardoned" his "feeble form."

And so, into this dull social-uplift tedium burst the stories of Gorky, lively, colorful, with their strong language and their daring heroes. "It is romanticism!" wrote the distressed Korolenko, Gorky's first "professor of technique" in the writing field. "It is romanticism, and that came to an end long ago . . . I feel as if you were not being yourself in your writing. You are a realist, not a romantic – a realist!"

It was indeed romanticism, and with all its fancy trappings, rather banal at that; Melchior de Vogué, who, along with André Gide, remains today the French critic who has probed deepest into the secrets of Russian literature, said as much in 1901. At a time when Gorky's success had become worldwide, Vogué recognized that his narratives were written "according to the conventional romantic pattern," and even if he was not able to understand their full social implication, at least Vogué must be credited with having raised the point: "It may be laden with literary and social consequence, this worn romanticism which returns to seek out, to pity, and to glorify Manfred and Rolla in the abyss where they have toppled."

Tolstoy himself had the same reaction. He noted in his journal that in Gorky "everything was imagined, artificial; mighty sentiments, heroic and false, but a tremendous talent." Chekhov expressed the same feeling when he said of Gorky's work, "It isn't written, it is performed." Korolenko, too, considered his "populist romanticism" to be "cerebral," invented out of nothing. The fact that he had quit the national tide of realism condemned Gorky in the eyes of these writers. Tolstoy told him when they met, ". . . somehow you are not Russian, your thoughts are not Russian."

Gorky had an original way of looking at the world. Not a child of the intelligentsia nor even of the moderately well-off common people, but born, like his heroes "in the back-alleys of life," into a brutal and illiterate setting, he possessed a thirst for learning and a respect for culture to a degree unknown among those for whom learning and culture had been, since childhood, their common lot. For the young boy, grandson of a Volga boatman, who had raised himself to the intellectual life by sheer hard work, the words beauty, ideal, joy, light had a vital significance. He fought his way to literature, animated by longings unknown to his contemporary writers.

In his essay *The Reader* (1898), Gorky explained his state of mind, criticizing contemporary literature and inviting the public to follow him along new, more colorful paths. "Everything in (it) is commonplace: commonplace people, commonplace thoughts, commonplace happenings! . . . Where is the challenge to creative living, where are the lessons of valor, where the words of encouragement giving wings to the soul?" And, turning to his ideal public, "We long to indulge in pretty fancies and daydreams and to be quaint and different . . ."

Gorky sought his first heroes (*Makar Chudra*, 1892, *Old Izergil*, 1893, *Malva*, 1897) among the gypsy nomads of the Black Sea, fishermen or peasants on the loose. Proud, passionate, living outside the society they scorned, they had their origins in Byron, by way of the early poems of Pushkin. Friends of the young Gorky have told how he filled thick notebooks with verses, and that he had a passion for Byron. But his characters were not merely Byronic; in their pride, their thirst for liberty, their heroic, bold action, one sensed the image of a new man. This impression was strengthened when the writer began to paint the same type of men, no longer in the setting of the steppe or the sea, but inhabiting damp cellars, outskirts of cities, ports, and flophouses. Men without allegiances but also without fetters, vagabonds – "bossiaks."

In literal translation, a "bossiak" is a barefoot tramp. But in Russian this word has the same sentimental ring as "hobo." According to Gorky, "the 'bossiak' is an intellectual among the half-men half-beasts, naked, vicious, starved, wronged by fate, inhabiting the festering slums of cities . . . a type of man worthy of attention who, by no means stupid, nurtures certain ambitions and should be viewed as a class."

The first bossiaks appeared in *Chelkash* and *Two Hobos* (1895). Gorky found their prototypes in the port of Odessa and among the tramps. Wild, bold, ready to throw to the winds the booty he had just stolen from under the noses of the customs officials at the risk of his life, Chelkash was portrayed in contrast to a dull, cowardly peasant, a prisoner of his own greed. Out of contempt, Chelkash hands over his booty to this man.

That was something original. Gorky dared to turn from the *muzhik*, the sainted, the good *muzhik*, martyr and accepted idol of democratic literature, preferring an outlaw, a bandit full of life, who knew how to enjoy freedom.

Then Gorky probed still deeper into the city, into the morose, dismal existence of its pariahs (*Orloff and His Wife, Konovalov*, 1897); but the novelty of his heroes saved him from the old realism. Men of good social position who had fallen and scorned money, peasants torn from the land and not yet rooted in the factories, unsuccessful students – these men were in constant flux, forming an unstable milieu in a state of revolt. They knew what it was they revolted against but not yet to what purpose. They had not found their place in society. Their torment was not something new to Russian literature, but now this torment gave forth a new sound.

The two hobos (from the story by that name) that the narrator encountered in the steppe had nothing more pressing to do than to sit down with him around a bottle of vodka and to start discoursing on their souls. And it was his starved soul which led Paul Goremyka (*Orphan Paul*), a foundling who had led an unbearable existence, to invest all his ideals in a prostitute. When the gap between reality and his dream dawned upon him, Paul murdered the woman and stood weeping over her body. Man-made justice sent him off to prison.

Konovalov (story by that name, 1897), a baker afflicted with bouts of drunkeness, was the most splendid figure in this gallery. This rough man with the eyes of a child said:

> There's nothing inside me to point the way. No spark in my soul – no strength perhaps. . . . It's just not there. . . . So I go on living and searching for that something, and longing for it, but what it is, I don't know. . . . There are lots of others like me. We're special people – don't fit into any picture.

The true social nature of this illiterate man came out when he is seen spending half his wages on books that attracted him, which he had the narrator read aloud. The story of the famous Cossack rebel of the seventeenth century, Stenka Razin, whose popular revolt foreshadowed the revolution, threw Konovalov into exaltation:

> It seemed that there were blood ties undissolved by the passage of three hundred years binding this tramp to Stenka. With all the force of his strong and vigorous body, with all the passion of a soul yearning for something "to point the way," he experienced the pain and wrath the freedom-loving rebel had known on being captured three centuries before.

The rock of Stenka Razin, on the Volga.

A conscious revolt – that was the "something" which Konovalov lacked. He never succeeded in conquering his depression, alcohol, nor the bog which was sucking him down. But he had a fleeting awareness of what was wrong. Fleeting, but so clear that one day out of hatred for his impotence, he hung himself in prison – they found him dangling from the air vent.

Before Gorky, his older contemporary, Chekhov, had sensed the positive social meaning of the "bossiak" phenomenon. His tramps (*Dremas*, 1888, *The Steppe*, 1888, *Thieves*, 1890), Merik, the horsethief, Dymov, who dreamed of the Siberian expanse, are also rebels. In one of his letters Chekhov wrote of these characters:

> It is not for religious schism, nor for vagrancy, nor for a sedentary life, but clearly for revolution that nature creates beings like the scoundrel Dymov . . . Only, there will never be a revolution in Russia and Dymov will end up by sinking into alcohol or will be sent to prison. He is a superfluous man.

There lies the profound difference between the two writers. Gorky believed in the revolution. His hobos and scamps were not "superfluous men," in classic Russian definition a literary type (*lichni cheloviek*). His tramps, just like his petrel, the bird of storms, are heralds of the future. Chekhov did not believe in the revolution, because he thought it could come only from the intellectuals; and he himself, whose principal heroes were intellectuals, painted them as having resigned from life. Gorky, on the contrary, awaited the revolution from the people; its power lay in them.

Such was the new sense which he infused into the stirring and romanticized picture of the bossiak. The Czarist censor realized it; the story *Konovalov* was found to be "very tendentious and harmful," "provocative," and "in many passages, tending towards socialism." The issue of the magazine in which it had been published was seized.

The social *élan* of the Gorkian hero was magnificently served by the author's language. Conventional and abounding in clichés as he strove for literary effect, his style acquired a spontaneity, a richness, a striking power of suggestion whenever his "people spoke." Other Russian writers of the nineteenth century had often given voice to the *muzhik*, but when Gorky's *muzhik* or bossiak raised his voice, all the other attempts, including Tolstoy's, seemed pale. Gorky was the people. Born in the heart of Russia, having worked at every trade, he knew all the popular speech and all the local slangs, including the composite language of the city slums, colored with butchered "erudite" expressions, full of the surprise of unexpected word endings and the vivid coarseness of improbable combinations. Gorky's knowledge of the resources of popular language was almost unlimited: slogans, maxims, puns, gibberish, oaths, rhymes and alliterations so cherished by the Russian learned, a supple, nimble vocabulary, ever giving birth to new forms. This linguistic fund (which Gorky was to abuse later on) heightened the originality of his work. Together with his fiery romanticism and his new type of pre-revolutionary hero, it made for an attractive novelty.

However, as we have noted, Gorky's colorful language was dulled whenever the characters yielded the floor to the narrator. What the British so aptly term "polite literature" was to be for Gorky something studied, not spontaneous. He had served his literary apprenticeship in a bad school; the cloak and dagger novel, the popular novel above all, had made up almost the sole reading of his adolescence, to the point where, after those grandiloquent flourishes, Xavier de Montépin, he said, seemed restrained. Chekhov warned him repeatedly against excesses of lyricism, accumulation of adjectives, and unnecessary big words. Gorky was never able to shed all his worn-out clichés, his stale comparisons, or his shaky grammar. As journalist, his energy very easily turned into brutality; as novelist, when he ceased to be completely plain, when he tried to "write," he plunged into banality. In addition, there were the constant repetitions. Even in what he liked most – descriptions of nature, the vast, sweeping landscapes of the immense Volga, the forests, the steppe – he was not always successful. It is enough to compare his tableaux with those of Turgenev to see just how much they are lacking in nuance. A Chekhov, conservative to the point of stinginess, is more successful in impressing us with the unexpected aspect of words and objects, which is the attribute of poetry. And in Gorky's work it is the poetry which is the weakest. He liked to write poetry – and did so poorly. In order to "justify" it, he frequently attributed it to his characters. It was a paradox that the extraordinary success of this young writer should have been due in good part to his bad poetry. Among the great Russian public which relished bad verse.

provided it carried an ideologic "content," his prose poems had an immense impact. "The Tale of an Earnest Heart," "The Story of the Falcon and the Eel" and, above all, "The Song of the Stormy Petrel," were welcomed as calls to the revolution. The famous refrain, "To the madness of the brave we sing our song!" became a real revolutionary rallying cry.

"It is doubtful," said one old Bolshevik, "that one can find in our literature a work which has had as many editions [as "The Song of the Stormy Petrel"]. It was printed and circulated in every city, hectographed and typed, copied by hand, and it was read and re-read by workers and students. . . ."

However, it was really bad poetry. The writer of *My Childhood* and *Strasti Mordasti*, the disturbing story of the little legless cripple and his bestiary of insects, was certainly a genuine poet; but he was determined to versify, with meter, with rhymes. . . .

It was not only in the colorful underworld that Gorky found his displaced men. His first novel, *Foma Gordeiev* (1899), which remains his best, introduces us into another social stratum, that of the merchants. From Ostrovski (1823-1886) – whose dramas showed the merchant families of the middle of the nineteenth century – to Gorky their description changed completely. With Ostrovski it was a powerful class, settled, stable, a solid block, "a sinister realm" which stifled any "ray of light," that is, the few pure figures who where quickly engulfed by the ignorance, the cupidity, and the cruel despotism of this class. In contrast to this, Gorky's merchants were men of the people who had succeeded in attaining wealth; they were still unsophisticated, full of contradictions, still restless and complicated. Gordeiev's father, Ignatius, "has three souls." Only "the first hinges on profits, gold, frantic work." But, "while he devoted so much energy to his pursuit of the ruble, he was not greedy in the strict sense of the word and occasionally it happened that he displayed an incomprehensible but sincere indifference towards his property." That would have been impossible for one of Ostrovski's characters. To throw away fistfuls of money in an outburst of debauchery – yes! but not to experience "a sincere indifference" toward it. That was the peculiarity of Ignatius' "second soul," "surly and malicious," the peculiarity of "the new man." As for his third soul, it "atoned."

A child was born to this man with three souls and his silent, mysterious wife, daugther of a Cossack Old Believer from the Urals; a son, Foma, who was always asking, "What's happening in me? Who am I?... Why can't I live like other people, sure and tranquil?... Where is my place?... What is my business?"

Ignorant and savage, a truly primitive force, Foma sought "release" in debauchery, alcohol, and foolery. One evening during an orgy on board a raft moored in the Volga, he reached the bank and, having detached the raft, sent his dumfounded companions into the eddies of the great river. Or another time on one of his own barges, he had the captain bound, and amused himself by ramming approaching light-barges and sinking them. He hurled himself "into the wild confusion of orgies, into the throng of people bewildered with stormy passions, half crazy with the longing to forget themselves." He wept when they sang mournful songs; bewildered, he threw himself into the dancing, sometimes flinging himself overboard into the water. Two or three times he caught sight of "the truth" but was unable to seize hold of it. One of the first times, taking part in the superhuman effort of the sailors who were righting one of the barges he had sunk, "a strange emotion took possession of Foma: he felt a passionate longing to pour himself into that excited roar of the workmen, broad and powerful as the river, into that irritating grate, into the shriek and scream of iron and the stormy splashing of the waves..." Drunk, self-forgetful, he tugged at the cable "experiencing for the first time in his life such a mighty inspiring sensation, and he gulped it down with all the force of his thirsty, hungry soul."

Another time, bursting with envy and longing, he attended the feast of some *real* workers, typographers, but was unsuccessful in mingling with them, in becoming one of them. He failed every test, until one day he suddenly understood that there would be no inner freedom for him as long as he held on to his wealth. So he threw his gold to the crowd, and then created a great scandal at an official banquet by shouting the dirty truth about themselves to the town dignitaries. Foma was considered crazy and he was put away. He ended up by apparently going out of his head and became a beggar, an enlightened vagabond.

What had happened to him? As he said himself: "A man goes down a river on a bark.... It may be a good bark, but under it the water is deep.... The bark is sturdy.... Yet if the man begins to feel the gloomy depth, no bark will save him. . . ."

Foma perished because he had begun "to sense the gloomy depth" of an upside-down world.

He was but the first of a series of such characters who were to appear repeatedly in the author's subsequent works: Matvei Kozhemyakin, Piotr Artamonov, certain figures from *Okurov Town*, or the portraits he lovingly drew of big industrialists and merchants like Bugrov and Morozov, those "white ravens" who, while exploiting their workers, gave money for revolutionary undertakings. "I know and I understand somewhat this type of man," said Gorky. "Each one of them has gone through a crisis [literally: "an upheaval of the soul"], painful, inevitable: this soul was born in the country, had grown up there in tranquility, and now in the city this pliable soul was being shaped by hundreds of tiny mallets, enlarging or contracting it."

Like the tramps, these stray merchants had lost their social position. They abounded in energy, which in itself was good, and which, properly utilized, could have regenerated the world; but finding no outlet, this force was turned back upon itself and was consumed in pointless destruction. The notion of pointless mischief is particularly Russian (despite *The Counterfeiters*), and they have a word for it which obviously cannot be translated – *ozorstvo*. It is not to be confused with the vandalism referred to as hooliganism (a term curiously enough borrowed from the English and having acquired wide acceptance in Russian). *Ozorstvo* is an old expression familiar in Russian epic poems of which one of the heroes, Vaska Buslaiev (Gorky made use of him) was the epitome of the *ozornik*, a brawler and a ravager; his soul was turned towards good, but not knowing how to find it, it floundered, damnably unfulfilled. Since the time of that cavalier of the *chanson de geste*, the word *ozorstvo* has been watered down and sometimes it is used to mean simply, naughty. But more often Gorky gave it its original sense. In one of his plays, a character complains that his vegetable gardens are being destroyed. "If only they had been driven by hunger," he says, "but no. . . ." "Angels don't eat, nor was Satan hungry when he rebelled against God," replied his friend. "That's exactly what I call ozorstvo," answered the first.

In one of his stories Gorky told how a typesetter, by inserting a vulgar sentence, distorted an article written by the editor-in-chief. The premeditated act of an awakened revolutionary? Hardly, since the hero simply felt "mischievous," "outraged," because his "soul was unhappy." The story is called *Ozornik* (The Insolent Man).

Gorky used this word repeatedly when speaking of Tolstoy.

"He had in him, I think, the inquisitive, mischievous wildness of a Vaska Buslaiev." And when on their first meeting Tolstoy began to ask him embarrassing questions, he wrote: "This is the *ozorstvo* of a gallant knight: Vaska Buslaiev, the *ozornik* of Novgorod, played just such pranks in his youth. Tolstoy is probing, constantly testing something, as if he were going to fight. It is interesting, but not much to my liking. He is the devil in person, and I am still a babe, and he should leave me alone."

There is in *ozorstvo* a tragic undertone, and it is in this sense that one poet characterized Rasputin as *staretz-ozornik* [old troublemaker]. The destructive actions of Gorky's heroes are a self-destruction, an atonement, an act of barbarism, surely, but a tragic act.

The turbulent life of these people had for its setting the broad, immense, magnificent sweep of the Volga, reflecting their thirst for the infinite. Gorky captured the essence of this landscape:

> On everything round rested the stamp of a certain sluggishness: everything – nature and people – lived awkwardly, lazily; but in this laziness there was a certain peculiar grace and, it would seem that behind the laziness was concealed a huge force, an unconquerable force, as yet unconscious of itself, not having, as yet, created for itself clear desires and aims.

The Volga's greatness left its mark on Gorky. Chaliapin, also born along the banks of the Volga, said it with assurance: "I know for sure, deeply, beyond any doubt, that all Gorky's ideas, all his feelings, all his acts, good or bad, had as their sole and unique source the Volga."

This was the river of Stenka Razin. A popular old ballad

sings of the Cossack chief sailing down the river laden with his booty, and hurling into the waters, as a sacrificial offering, his lovely captive, a Persian princess: "Volga, Volga, our mother, accept this gift from a Don Cossack."

Ignatius Gordeiev acted no differently. From the river bank, carried away with joy, he saw his own barge smashed to smithereens by the cracking ice. Although his barge was brand new, he rejoiced and cried to the river, "Give it to her . . . now again . . . squeeze – crush! . . . But just see how the Volga is working! Mother Volga can rend the whole earth apart. . . . Well, what's the use of being sorry? . . . The Volga gave and the Volga has taken away."

And it was also on the banks of the Volga that, two years after Gorky, Lenin was born.

LOUD-SPEAKER OF THEATER

The tremendous vitality of Gorky's heroes and the dramatic nature of their conflicts were made to order for the stage. The directors of the Moscow Art Theater, Stanislavsky and Nemirovitch-Danchenko, enthusiastically urged the young author to write for the theater. Adapters, too, felt the dramatic possibilities of his novels. In 1901 alone, the Committee on Censorship received 31 adaptations of *Foma Gordeiev*, some of which were played in the provinces and even, in Petersburg, in two theaters at one time. With their stress on the "defiant" speeches, these adaptations emphasized the figure of the worker, however minor it might have been in the novel.

Thanks to the stirring power of direct contact with the public, Gorky's new man took on an enhanced resonance on the stage – making the theater a revolutionary tool *par excellence*. The emotional and political influence of Gorky's plays was increased by the fact that they were produced by the Moscow Art Theater, the newly created (1898) theater of the progressive intelligentsia, which sought to renovate art and thinking. Chekhov was its great dramatist, and his *Seagull* became the very symbol of the Art Theater. In Moscow, during the 1902 season, it was said that Gorky's passionate falcon had come to join Chekhov's nostalgic gull.

Chekhov's dramaturgy carried on the traditions of Ibsen's theater and, above all, Hauptmann's, which dealt with the state of the human mind. But it substituted for the somber grandeur of Scandinavia and the fantasy of Germany, the monotony of provincial Russian daily life. It was from Ibsen and Hauptmann that Chekhov, and through him Gorky, borrowed the substance of the technique in which the action gave way to something in the nature of parallel monologues which never became dialogues, each person pursuing his own thoughts in phrases which he seemed to be addressing to himself. The pauses and the silences were as loaded with meaning as the responses. Aware of the lack of "action" – the very essence of theater – Gorky considered himself "a wretched playwright," as did Chekhov. He was so uncertain of his craft that he generally designated his dramatic works "scenes," and it took the authority of a Nemirovitch-Danchenko to force him to call *Vassa Geleznova* a "play." Tormented by doubt, Gorky reworked them endlessly and there are frequently two versions extant.

In any event, his drama had a tremendous success, due perhaps less to its art than to its reality. Its characters expressed the state of mind of the Russian public at the turn of the century: the melancholy of the circles whose historic role was to end with the revolution of 1917. But Gorky, with his new heroes, "arrogant and unbroken," added the promise of a new hope. In fact, the impact of his plays is more interesting than the plays themselves.

In *Smug Citizens*, a conflict in the heart of a family of tradespeople of the old society, the new man is Nil, the railway worker, for the first time a "real" worker, who, according to the author, represented "a man with a calm belief in his strength and in his right to rebuild life according to his own judgment." To tell the truth, he was somewhat one-dimensional, seen only from the outside; but the play came out at a time of great political tension. At first all production of it was refused, and then cuts were required.

Concerning these cuts, the police records reveal an interesting note addressed by the Minister of the Interior to the Governor-General of Moscow, proposing that he "appoint a person specially directed to attend the dress rehearsal, with the purpose of drawing up an official report on the theatrical impact produced by Gorky's first dramatic effort. In this way it might be possible to prevent the recitation in public of pas-

Gorky surrounded by the actors of the Moscow Art Theater. (*Smug Citizens*, 1902)

sages or expressions which on reading do not give a negative impression, but which on the stage might produce an undesirable effect."

Thanks to the snobbery of the influential ladies of Petersburg high society, in all probability, authorization for the play was accorded, but only for four performances on subscribers' evenings, in front of a "safe" public. The Art Theater decided to hold the premier in Petersburg itself, on March 26, 1902, during one of its tours there. But the authorities demanded a "special" dress rehearsal. Nemirovitch-Danchenko related:

> With incredible speed, fashionable society was informed and we were swamped by requests for orchestra boxes and stalls, from the families of important functionaries and the diplomatic service. The production drew a sparkling audience, refined and politically influential, such as would have compared very favorably with a European gathering.

Beforehand, on several evenings during which Ibsen's *Enemy of the People* was being played, Nemirovitch-Danchenko climbed up to "heaven" – where the seats were distributed free to students – in order to persuade this restless audience to refrain from any demonstration. The overly cautious police replaced the ushers with their own agents.

The Petersburg premiere was followed by the one in Moscow, but in neither of the capitals did the spectacle bring the anticipated success. That was to come to Gorky several months later, in December, 1902, with *The Lower Depths.*

This time the subject matter was more colorful, and the

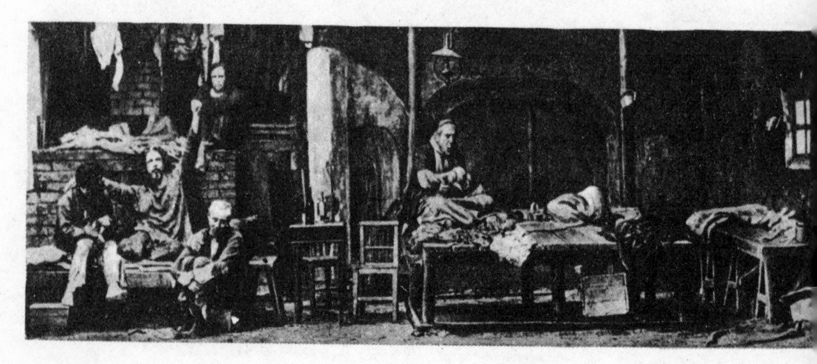

The Lower Depths, at the Moscow Art Theater. (Scene from Act IV.)

Poster for the Moscow Art Theater, "December 18, 1902 first showing, *The Lower Depths*." "Tickets by subscription only."

МОСКОВСКІЙ ХУДОЖЕСТВЕННЫЙ ТЕАТРЪ

Среда, 18-го Декабря.

Въ 1-й разъ:

НА ДНѢ,

сцены въ 4-хъ дѣйствіяхъ, соч. **Максима Горькаго.**

Участвующіе: Г. С. Бурджаловъ, Е. П. Муратова, М. Ө. Андреева, В. Ө. Грибунинъ, А. П. Харламовъ, А. Л. Загаровъ, М. Г. Савицкая, О. Л. Книпперъ, М. А. Самарова, В. В. Лужскій, К. С. Станиславскій, В. И. Качаловъ, М. А. Громовъ, И. М. Москвинъ, А. И. Адашевъ, Н. А. Барановъ, А. Л. Вишневскій и др.

Декораціи художника **В. А. Симова.**

НАЧАЛО ВЪ 8 ЧАС. ВЕЧ., ОКОНЧ. ВЪ 12 ЧАС. НОЧИ.

БИЛЕТЫ ВСѢ ПРОДАНЫ.

Четвергъ, 19-го Декабря, во 2-й разъ: **НА ДНѢ.**
(Билеты всѣ проданы).

Пятница, 20-го Декабря, въ 16-й разъ: **ВЛАСТЬ ТЬМЫ.**

Суббота, 21-го Декабря, въ 3-й разъ: **НА ДНѢ.**

Репертуаръ спектаклей съ 26-го Декабря 1902 г. по 6-е [illegible] **афишами.**

theme absolutely new to the stage: the depiction of a flophouse and its inhabitants, old aristocrats mingling with men of the people, fallen, complex, and passionate. In the time between plays the troupe had at last surmounted the difficulties that Gorky's style presented, chief among which, according to Stanislavsky, was "the super-clever and highflown ludicrous sermonizing. . . ." It was a matter of putting across

> a new tone, a new style of acting, a new realism, a special romanticism, a pathos bordering at the same time on theatrical affectation and preaching. You have to know how to speak Gorky's language, to make his sentences ring, to make them come alive. You have to be able to recite simply his sermonizing, didactic monologues, without letting the theatrical artificiality give a falseness to the natural vigor. If not, there is the danger of falling into melodrama.

Smug Citizens having caused the police no difficulty, they authorized the production of *The Lower Depths* (after many precautions to be sure) "because [the police] expected the play to flop with a thud." But they were misinformed. Moscow had been in a fever of waiting for *The Lower Depths* ever since Gorky's reading of it before the company of actors and other artists. To one actor's question about what effect the author would want to obtain, Gorky had answered: "If you do no more than succeed in shaking the spectator so that he is uncomfortable in his seat, I will be very happy."

> The production [wrote Stanislavsky] was a huge success. There were countless curtain calls for the directors and the actors, and for the playwright himself. Gorky was comic to behold when he appeared for the first time upon the platform, a cigarette between his lips (he had forgotten to put it out), smiling, completely bewildered and not aware that he was supposed to bow . . . . Gorky became the hero of the day. They followed him in the streets and to the theater; crowds of admirers, especially women, gathered around him; at first, embarrassed by his popularity, he made an awkward appearance, pulling on his short red mustache, constantly smoothing with his strong, masculine hands the stiff locks of his long hair, or tossing back his head. Disconcerted, he trembled, hunched over and his nostrils quivering, so great was his befuddlement. "My children!," he said to his fans with a guilty smile. "Listen . . . this is so embarrassing. . . . Honestly! Upon my word! . . . Why should you look at me? I'm not a singer . . . a dancer. . . . A fine thing! Come now, see here, really! . . ." But this comic bewilderment and his unusual manner of expressing himself in his con-

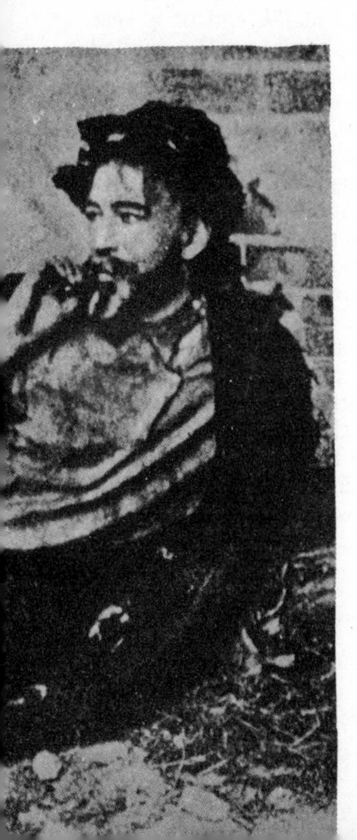

The Lower Depths. Stanislavsky in the role of Satin.

fusion only served to augment the interest in him, and the number of his followers. Gorky's charm was forceful. He had a beauty all his own, a way about him, a spontaneity.

Smug Citizens, following its Russian premiere in March, 1902, was played in Berlin and Vienna that December. *The Lower Depths* crossed the frontier even more quickly. But it was provincial Russia which reacted with the most dramatic furor, to such an extent that the censor applied a very severe measure to both plays: special authorization had to be requested for any performance in the provinces, to be played according to an *ad hoc* censored text; productions of the *The Lower Depths* were forbidden in the popular theaters and in any other language of the Empire than Russian. Nevertheless the plays had numerous productions in the various cities.

The Lower Depths remains Gorky's greatest and the most long-lived dramatic success, and, indeed, the only one. It had a great success in the bookstores, too; the first edition of 40,000 copies was exhausted in two weeks, and at the end of a year it had sold over 75,000 copies. Never before in Russia had there been a success of such dimensions.

The plays which followed had only limited interest. The most notable was *Summer People* (1904), in which the conflict between two groups of the intelligentsia was welcomed by the public like a political meeting. During its production in Petersburg, the monarchistic members of the audience tried to create a disturbance, but the democrats won out and gave the author, who was present in the theater, an ovation. At the time of his detention in the Peter and Paul fortress, January-February 1905, Gorky wrote *Children of the Sun*, which he himself considered an absolute failure. It caused a stir however, having given rise to some incidents with political repercussions.

In story, in novel, and on stage, Gorky's heroes brought a revival, thanks above all to his romanticism, which the author defined as – "an active attitude before life, a glorification of labor, a training in the will to live, an enthusiasm for building new forms of life, a hatred for the old world."

THE CALL OF THE REVOLUTION

Gorky's childhood and youth, as he himself has related, coincided with the awakening of Russia and with its preparation for the upheaval of 1905. The cities along the Volga, his native region, large river ports and industrial centers, familiarized the boy not only with the world of the workers but also with the world of the revolutionaries – those deportees and former political prisoners that the government was driving from the capitals. They were so numerous as to form an actual class. It was in this atmosphere that young Gorky became aware of the imminence of the revolution. How could he not have wished for it, this grandson of a serf and a Volga boatman, condemned to earn his own living from the age of ten? "You say – a Marxist!" he was to write. "I dare say, however, not according to Marx, but because my hide was tanned that way. More and better than from books, I learned Marxism at the side of Semenov, a Kazan baker."

The university town of Kazan was one of the main centers of political ferment. In turn stevedore, gardener, music-hall singer, and above all baker, working under terribly rough conditions, it was there in Kazan, alongside the students and in the underground Marxist circles, that Gorky began his political training. One of the centers of activity was Derenkov's grocery

Kazan in the nineteenth century; entrance to the city.

and bakery shop, which concealed behind a screen a library of proscribed books. Gorky was both a baker of bread and a conspirator.

He acquired his new knowledge in snatches. Greedily he gulped down the popular political and scientific literature. Intoxicated with the prospects spreading before him, he sustained an unwavering faith, so to speak of a religious nature, in the power of progress and reason. This acquisition of knowledge was not easy. Our self-educated baker was painfully aware of the vast gap which separated him from the student youths for whom he was a kind of curiosity. In 1887, when he was 19, despairing of ever bridging the gap, he shot himself in the chest with a revolver. The bullet merely pierced a lung. They saved him, but this wound was the source of his tuberculosis.

Gorky's political education continued, haphazardly and unsystematically, at first by the side of Romas, an exile returned from Siberia who agitated among the peasants; and then, in the circles of deportees working on the Tsaritsyn (now Stalingrad) railroad. Although familiar with Marxism, he did not take to it all at once. Having organized a study circle in the little town of Krutaia, made up of two telegraphers, a mechanic, a woodworker, a printer-bookbinder, he attempted with his companions a Tolstoyan experiment of return to primitive happiness in an agricultural colony. This was the period of Tolstoy's ascendancy, and it was to be a long while before Gorky would come to condemn as ill-omened the influence of that "man with the solved problems."

But then, Alexei Peshkov was 21, and it was over his signature that the Krutaia group wrote to Tolstoy in all sincerity: "It is said that you possess a great deal of uncultivated land. We are asking you for one piece." As the answer was slow in

Tsaritsyn on the Volga (later Stalingrad).

Kazan, 1887.

coming, Alexei was charged by his comrades to make the trip to Yasnaya Polyana, about 660 miles away, part of which he traveled on foot. The master was not there, he pushed on to Moscow in the hope of finding him in the city, but there he was firmly turned away by Countess Tolstoy.

Back in Nizhni Novgorod, where the colony of exiles had continued to expand, he met two old acquaintances from Kazan: Chekin, the schoolteacher who had been retired because he was suspect, and Somov, the former Siberian deportee. He moved in with them and as his companions were already under "a discreet surveillance" by the police, it was extended to cover Gorky. This surveillance seemed to the police all the more justified because Gorky was working in a tavern washing and corking bottles, or rolling casks all day long – he was not an intellectual but a real worker, and this was serious. A hearing was held on him and from that day forth the dossier on Alexei Peshkov began to grow. During October, 1889, Somov was arrested in connection with the discovery of an illegal printing press. His roommates were questioned and the inspector's report noted that "Peshkov conducted himself with insolence and impertinence during the interrogation." He was arrested but questioning failed to turn up anything against him, except that "in Kazan Peshkov worked in a bakery set up for disloyal purposes; was acquainted there with disloyal persons, . . . read books of a certain not quite desirable nature, not quite

Nizhni Novgorod prison where Alexei was held for the first time in 1889.

Nizhni Novgorod on the Volga (later Gorky), around the middle of the nineteenth century.

corresponding to his intellectual level and the education he had received. . . ."

But Gorky was set free: at that time "suspicious ideas" were not sufficient to justify imprisonment – besides, the time for the drawing was approaching and he was sure to be chosen for military service. He felt so lost and so alone that in a way he looked forward to that possibility as an escape. But the army doctor wanted no part of a man "with a hole in his lung." In his distress, Gorky asked to be made a member of a topographical mission which was going to Pamir, but for their part, this group would have nothing to do with a "political suspect."

So he turned to literature. To Korolenko, the writer, who, after ten years of Siberian exile was confined to Nizhni, Gorky submitted what he considered "an excellent poem in verse and prose," "The Song of the Old Oak." Alexei met with severe criticism. Crushed, he temporarily left literature and soon after took leave of Nizhni to wander on foot across the south of Russia. For almost two years he roamed the region of the Don, the Ukraine, Bessarabia as far as the Danube, returning along the coast of the Black Sea until, crossing the Crimea, he reached the Caucasus. He worked here and there, sharing the life of gypsies, fishermen, stevedores, and hobos from the port of Odessa. He hired himself out as a laborer on a railroad-building project and went through many adventures.

Finally settled in Tiflis at the home of an exile, he found a hospitable revolutionary milieu of students and workers. Now he became the teacher. Kaliuzhni, active in the famous "Will of the People" group, urged Alexei to write and helped him to publish his first story, *Makar Chudra*, in the local newspaper, *Caucasus*. September 12 (24 in the modern calendar), 1892, the day of its publication, the author considered the date of his entry into the literary arena. It was in the newspaper office that, pressed for a signature, he hit upon his pseudonym. Henceforth Alexei Peshkov gave way to Maxim Gorky.

In the autumn he rediscovered his first love, Madame Kaminskaia, the wife of an exile, who this time followed him to Nizhni. Back in his native village, Gorky worked as a clerk in a lawyer's office, meanwhile stepping up his contributions to the provincial press, and soon also to that of Moscow. He moved to the Volga town of Samara, where Korolenko had obtained for him a regular column in the *Samara Gazette*. For him it was a gold mine. He received a fixed salary of 100

Issue of *Caucasus*,
September 12, 1892

Суббота 12-го сентября 1892 г.

Годъ горовъ седьмой

№ 242

ТИФЛИСЪ

КАВКАЗЪ

МАКАРЪ ЧУДРА.

Съ моря дулъ влажный и холодный вѣтеръ, разнося по степи задумчивую мелодію плеска набѣгавшей на берегъ волны и шелеста прибрежныхъ кустовъ. Изрѣдка его порывы приносили съ собой иззябшіе, сморщенные и желтые листья и бросали ихъ въ костеръ, раздувая пламя, отчего окружавшая насъ мгла осенней ночи вздрагивала и, пугливо отодвигаясь, открывала на мигъ слѣва—безграничную степь, справа—безконечное море и прямо противъ меня

...аю, а потомъ ляжетъ въ нее и сгніетъ въ ней. Ничего по немъ не останется, ничего онъ не видитъ съ своего поля и умираетъ, какъ родился, дуракомъ.

Чтожъ, онъ родился за тѣмъ, что-ли, чтобъ поковырять землю, да и умереть, не успѣвъ даже могилы самому себѣ выковырять? Вѣдома ему воля? Ширь степная понятна? Говоръ морской волны веселитъ ему сердце? Эге! Онъ рабъ какъ только родился и во всю жизнь рабъ, да и все тутъ! Что онъ съ собой можетъ сдѣлать? Только удавиться, коли поумнѣетъ немного.

А я, вотъ смотри, въ 58 лѣтъ столько видѣлъ, что коли написать все это

о чемъ-... ли кон... страст... савица ... голосъ ... какъ-т... тельно ... говори... матов... рицы, ... нью т... знаніе ... красота ... она са...

Мака...

rubles a month plus three kopeks for each line of prose fiction, with the obligation of turning in a story every Sunday.

It was certainly a gold mine, at last an assured existence, but there he was, a literary hack. He was obliged to write on local matters, to feed on rumors, gossip, scandal, and to interest himself in municipal administration, in the local horse-car and in thefts. Adopting his favorite tone of grim cynicism, he signed these news stories with a facetious alias, Jehudill Chlamida, thus sparing the name of Gorky. At the least, he tried to bring out the social aspect of issues, and came forward as a friend of justice in his stories. "I was disgusted with the mayor, the bishop, the town, and a whole bunch of other things." Sometimes he succeeded in publicizing the exploitation of the laborers, workmen's accidents, injustices and lies, thereby preparing himself for social journalism on a much larger scale.

In October of 1896, Gorky fell ill with tuberculosis. With aid from the Literary Fund he left for a cure in the Crimea; then, pursued by the police, settled for a little while in the Ukraine in a milder climate, and in 1898 after some wandering, he returned to Nizhni, his home base.

Ever since *The Song of the Falcon* (1895), welcomed as a hymn to the revolution, the name of Gorky had been on everybody's lips; and in 1898, the publication of two volumes of his stories enjoyed a great success. The police, uneasy, watched him closely, but he moved about too much and they couldn't follow him. An 1898 report said:

> He is an extremely suspicious man; he has read a lot, he has a fine handwriting, he has traveled throughout almost all of Russia (most often on foot); he spent nearly a year in Tiflis without any precise occupation and has left there for no one knows where. . . .

They finally found him again in Nizhni and on May 5, 1898, the police took him back to Tiflis, the original scene of his suspicious doings. He was put in a cell in the Metek prison. Then, returned once again to Nizhni Novgorod, he became the cynosure of that part of Russia "which was stirring." He gave himself over to great activity, especially of a social nature. But politics called out to him. The government had issued, by way of warning, a "provisional ruling" which provided for drafting into the army "students guilty of group disorders." This

Nizhni Novgorod, 1896.

measure was applied in Kiev, in December, 1900, to some hundred students who had taken part in a rally. Gorky wrote letters, called for resistance. The following spring he was in Petersburg. A short time before, he had been feted by his editors and some of the most celebrated authors and journalists in the capital, and had caused a scandal by his coarseness and scorn for convention. On March 4, 1901, he took part in the famous student demonstration in front of the Cathedral of Our Lady of Kazan in Petersburg, a demonstration which the Cossacks and the mounted police turned into a massacre. As the government gave out a garbled version of the incident, Gorky signed a protest of the intellectuals against the police violence. He was believed by the police to have been the author of the pamphlet, but there was no proof. The police were, therefore, only too happy when several weeks later they were able to arrest Gorky on the charge of having mimeographed pamphlets intended for the industrial suburb of Sormovo (where, the following May 1, an uprising took place which Gorky later described in *The Mother*). Gorky was placed under house arrest in Arzamas, a small town only a short distance from Nizhni. But a recurrence of tuberculosis won him permission to return to the Crimea. As he had to pass through Moscow, he was to be allowed a week's time there in order to make personal contact with the Art Theater, for which he was preparing *Smug Citizens.* But just before his departure, there was another incident. A local correspondent wrote it up in Lenin's paper, *Iskra*:

> On November 7, 1901, Maxim Gorky left Nizhni for the Crimea. His departure has stirred up our peaceful swamp, no doubt for a long time to come. The liberal intelligentsia, lawyers, doctors, etc., decided to arrange a farewell dinner for Gorky and to deliver an address in his honor. The young people as well, for their part, wanted to participate in the "banquet" and to seize the occasion to show the bourgeois intelligentsia that it has nothing in common with those who intended to raise an active and vigorous protest against the regime.

The banquet gathered together some 150 persons. The address by the liberals was vague and pompous; the one by the students' called for struggle. Gorky replied bearishly, superbly,

Nizhni Novgorod, 1898.

aligning himself with the youth against his bourgeois admirers. He read aloud *About a Writer Who Became Conceited,* a pamphlet which he had drawn up following the scandal of his reception in Petersburg. In it he called himself and his readers to account: "It is not good for a writer to have many fans. Men who have anything to do with the 'public' must disinfect the atmosphere with the help of the acid of truth." A furor broke out among those present and the police hastened his departure by serving him with an order of expulsion; hundreds of young people carried him in triumph to the station, and organized noisy demonstrations there and in the city. Authorization was withdrawn for his sojurn in Moscow. Just before arriving in the capital, his coach was detached and brought back 33 miles to the little town of Podolsk, where the writer had to await the train connection for the Crimea. His friends, who awaited him in vain in the Moscow station, took the suburban train and rushed to Podolsk – among them, Gorky's editor, his German translator, Chaliapin, and Bunin. A noisy dinner was arranged much to the displeasure of the gendarmerie, and when, late at night, his friends accompanied Gorky to the station where the express was to make a special stop to pick him up, the whole town was on the platform and the harassment by the authorities wound up in a grand finale.

The biting pages of *About a Writer Who Became Conceited* were welcomed as a choice morsel by the underground press. Students rejoiced over them at their meetings. Even greater was the impact of *Springtime Melodies*, on the whole a rather mild satire on government morality; it was the censor's suppression of it which made it exciting. However, "through inadvertence" the censor let the most powerful fragment of it slip through, "The Song of the Stormy Petrel"! Gorky wrote: "I delivered the rough draft to the student group of Muscovites deported to Nizhni; they busied themselves making copies of the text and distributing it."

By that time Gorky was famous. His rather unpolished behavior only added to his renown and gave rise to many anecdotes. And, in fact, here was a writer whose physical ap-

With Chaliapin, 1902.

pearance corresponded marvelously to the legend. Suits were unbecoming to him, but he was splendid in his black peasant blouse; tall, thin, slightly hunched, with his boots, his little mustache and his unruly head of hair. A charming smile, a soft, deep voice, a Volga pronunciation stressing the "o" which

The "Wednesdays," liberal democratic literary group of Moscow: l. to r., Skitalets, Andreyev, Gorky, Teleshov, Chaliapin, Bunin (1902).

sounded "exotic" in the capital cities. And – shades of romanticism! – he was tubercular.

In the spring of 1902 a tremendous scandal came along to intensify the writer's popularity.

The Imperial Academy of Sciences elected Gorky Honorary Academician in belles-lettres. Having learned of this decision which appeared in the Official Gazette of March 1, 1902, Nicholas II wrote in the margin, "More than odd!" and expressed his disapproval in a letter to the Minister of Education.

Once again the opposite result was achieved. Chekhov and Korolenko, Honorary Academicians, resigned in sympathy with Gorky, and the latter was more than ever acclaimed by public opinion.

We come now to the crucial year of 1905. The first few days found Petersburg in a state of agitation. The workers, supported by the priest, Gapon, decided to hold, on January 9 (22), a "march on the Winter Palace." They wanted to appeal to the Czar about their miserable conditions. But the government, badly informed or pretending to be, prepared reprisals. This was the famous massacre, in front of the Winter Palace, of unarmed men led by a priest, which was to go down in history as "Bloody Sunday."

Stunned, Gorky that evening drew up a declaration, *A call to all Russian citizens and to the public opinion of the states of Europe,* and submitted the draft to the members of the delegation. The following day, in the course of a search, the police found the document and very easily identified the handwriting. On January 11, Gorky was incarcerated in the Peter and Paul fortress.

The police began a painstaking collection of "evidence," but unexpected opposition developed in a mass uprising of public opinion. This threat showed itself with such spontaneity, speed, and violence as to confound the imperial government – more especially as the European newspapers joined with the Russian press. On February 20, 1905, the writer was released on bail (10,000 rubles paid out by his publishers). But the Okhrana (secret police) soon announced that his presence was responsible

Болѣе чѣмъ оригинально!

Правительственный Вѣстникъ

Пятница 1 Марта 1902 г. № 48.

* Въ состоявшемся 21-го минувшаго февраля соединенномъ засѣданіи отдѣленія русскаго языка и словесности Императорской академіи наукъ и разряда изящной словесности закрытою баллотировкою шарами были произведены, согласно съ существующими постановленіями, выборы въ почетные академики разряда изящной словесности. Избранными оказались: Александръ Васильевичъ Сухово-Кобылинъ и Алексѣй Максимовичъ Пѣшковъ («Максимъ Горькій»).

for constant agitation, and he was transferred to Riga. There, he immediately set about assembling material on the events of January 9. Government circles gradually realized that it would be preferable to stifle the whole business. But Gorky would not hear of it. He wanted at all cost to be tried.

> The tribunal will be for me, and shame will fall upon the Romanovs and Company. If there is a conviction and I am sentenced, I will have a fine opportunity of explaining to Europe why I stand up against the "regime in power," the regime that slaughters peaceful and unarmed citizens and children, and why I am a revolutionary.

Thus warned, the government decided first to hold a closed hearing; then deferred the matter, hoping to let it blow over; and finally wiped it out through an act of amnesty, on the occasion of the political reform of October, 1905, and the granting of the Constitution.

During the brief "days of freedom" Gorky participated in the creation of the first legal Bolshevik daily, *New Life (Novaia Zhizn* – editor-in-chief, Lenin). It was there that his famous

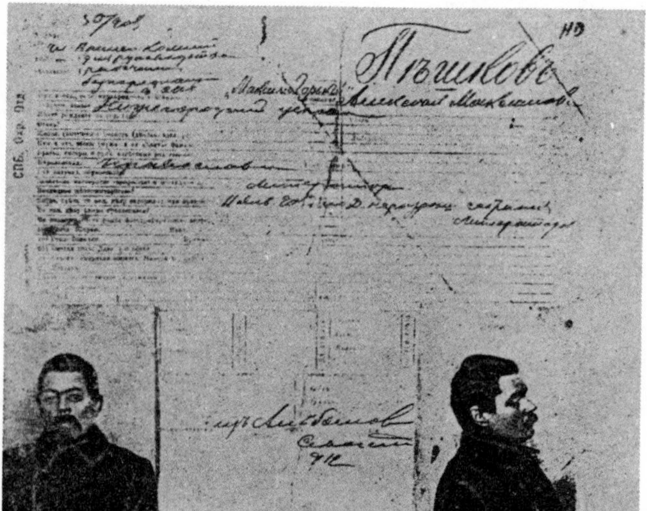

Notes on the Petty-Bourgeois Mentality * appeared, which brought the liberals down on him but won him Lenin's increasing attention.

The constitutional dawn faded rapidly. During those frantic months, Gorky took part in feverish revolutionary activity, publishing, delivering public speeches, and participating in the armed Moscow uprising. The police continued to watch him, and his friends, in order to prevent his arrest – this time in an atmosphere of the blackest reaction – decided to send him to the United States where he would be able, thanks to his fame and his propagandistic talents, to solicit for the Social-Democratic party treasury. In January, 1906, Gorky secretly crossed the Finnish frontier.

* This title is given in American texts as *Notes on Smugness* or *Notes on Philistinism.*

The file on Alexei Peshkov, alias Maxim Gorky, in the Petersburg police department.

GORKY AND THE WEST

Gorky was no stranger to Europe or to the United States. After 1899 his works had been translated into several languages. In 1901 they appeared through six German publishing houses, and in France, Melchior de Vogué had written a study of the writer which excited world-wide interest. *The Lower Depths* was performed mainly on the European stage. At the time of Gorky's escape from Russia to Berlin, the Moscow Art Theater was touring with this play; and in the Berlin theaters Max Reinhardt was staging *The Lower Depths* and *Children of the Sun*. The windows of bookstores displayed his works and his photographs. In his honor, Reinhardt organized a public evening. When Gorky came out on the stage, the audience – containing numerous Russian political emigrés – stood up to welcome him, shouting *hoch*! Karl Liebknecht, the future leader of German communism, came up to Kachalov, the celebrated actor of the Art Theater, and told him to take a look "over in one corner of the menagerie in the auditorium itself"; hidden behind the curtains of a box seat were the sons of Wilhelm II, including the Crown Prince.

From Berlin Gorky proceeded to Paris. That spring, 1906, the Russian government, ruined by the disastrous Russo-Japanese War and shaken by revolutionary pressure, was negotiating with the Western states a loan intended to aid it in bolstering its internal situation. Gorky's assigned mission was to raise Western public opinion against the loan. On April 9, 1906, *L'Humanité* (Jean Jaurès' newspaper) published his appeal – "Not One Penny for the Russian Government!" – wholeheartedly supported by the Society of Friends of the Russian People whose membership included Anatole France, Steinlen, Mirbeau, Langlois, and Seighnobos. Still, the French banks, with government approval, awarded the loan and Gorky, disappointed and indignant, wrote his violent pamphlet *La Belle France,* which won him the severe criticism of certain French journalists. A year before they had come to his defense while he was imprisoned in the Peter and Paul fortress – and now, here he was jeering at their country! Gorky replied with two letters published in *L'Humanité* on December 11, 1906, entitled, "To My Detractors." One of these letters, tempered and regretful in tone, was addressed to Aulard; the other, vehement and scornful, was to Gérault-Richard, René Viviani, Jules Claretie, and others.

Employing every means, the Czarist government tried to hinder Gorky's entry into the United States. The Russian ambassador to Washington sought to have the American law forbidding the entry of "anarchists" into the country invoked against him. But the Immigration Department at that time, respecting the Constitution and civil liberties, refused to classify Gorky as such. Unable, therefore, to count on the authorities, the ambassador gambled on American prudishness, with greater success. With the help of the chain of dailies already belonging to Hearst, he made it known that the woman accompanying the writer was not his legal wife. The couple was driven away from one hotel after another, but the maneuver worked in Gorky's favor, giving him tremendous publicity. Madame Andreyeva and he, seated on their suitcases in the street, surrounded by fascinated newspapermen, were finally taken into a "commune" on Staten Island at the home of a couple named Martin.

However, the success of Gorky's mission was compromised. Naturally, he had some friends, but most of the American intellectuals, virtuous people, viewed him with anything but satisfaction. Mark Twain refused to preside at a banquet in his honor. The amount of money raised was insignificant – some ten thousand dollars.

A MES DÉTRACTEURS !

DEUX LETTRES DE MAXIME GORKI

L'emprunt de Judas. — L'enseignement de la Révolution française. — Réponse à des insulteurs. — Socialiste et bourgeois.

Notre éminent camarade Maxime Gorki nous adresse ces deux lettres en réponse aux attaques virulentes dont il a été l'objet à propos de son article sur la « belle France », attaques qu'il n'a connues que tout récemment à son arrivée d'Amérique.

I

Lettre à M. Aulard

Cher Maître,

Dans l'amas de paroles injurieuses, fruits d'une irritation impuissante, dans les éclaboussures de boue et le plat bavardage par lesquels la presse française a répondu à ce que j'avais écrit sur la dernière action déshonorante de la France financière et gouvernementale, j'ai vu avec étonnement et avec tristesse votre honorable nom, cher professeur

Votre livre sur la lutte épique du peuple français contre la tyrannie est lu par le prolétariat russe qui y puise la science de se sacrifier et de mourir pour la liberté, dont il a besoin autant que d'air. Mon estime pour le grand historien que vous etes est si profonde que je ne peux pas laisser sans répondre votre article relatif à « la belle France ». Je ne le peux pas, car pour moi, l'essentiel, c'est moins ce que les autres pensent de moi que ce que j'en pense moi-même.

Vous n'avez évidemment pas lu mon article tout entier. Malgré cela, vous reconnaissez qu'en partie au moins j'avais d'assez solides motifs pour m'indigner. Cela, vous devez le reconnaître pleinement, cher professeur !

En effet, il ne s'agit pas seulement de ce que, comme vous le dites, « sans l'argent français, le tsar n'aurait pas pu dissoudre la Douma », non ! Il s'agit plutôt de ce que, sans cet argent maudit, on n'aurait pas versé si abondamment et si férocement le sang du peuple russe. Et, que vous le vouliez ou non, ce sang a taché d'une tache honteuse la face des bourgeois et du gouvernement français qui a permis cet emprunt de Judas.

Ce n'est certainement pas la presse bourgeoise qui effacera cette tache ; elle-même n'est pas assez propre pour cela.

Vous vous trompez aussi en supposant que j'avais lancé mon reproche à la face de la France tout entière. Pourquoi me croire si naïf ? Je sais que le peuple n'est jamais responsable de la politique des classes dirigeantes et du gouvernement, leur laquais fidèle. Je connais en particulier le peuple français qui a semé partout en Europe les

vous commencez à traiter la logique, la vérité et la noble langue française, tout comme, en Russie, les cosaques traitent les femmes. L'oppression, voyez-vous, est abjecte parce qu'elle déprave des étrangers et des indifférents eux-mêmes, comme cela a été votre cas.

Je ne réponds jamais aux insinuations dirigées contre ma personne. Plus elles sont grossières, plus tôt je les oublie. Mais vous m'accusez de manquer de sentiments de gratitude, Messieurs, et je suis obligé de m'expliquer là-dessus.

Vous dites : « Nous nous sommes levés pour prendre la défense de Gorki lors de son emprisonnement, et lui... »

Permettez-moi de vous donner un bon conseil : Si par mégarde, par imprudence ou pour une autre cause, vous avez une fois donné libre cours à vos sentiments d'humanité, eh bien ! ne vous en vantez pas ! Ce n'est pas beau...

« Je fus bon vis-à-vis de toi, tu dois me payer pour cela par ta gratitude », voilà ce qui ressort de vos paroles. Mais, messieurs, je n'éprouve pas de reconnaissance pour vous, et votre générosité, j'estime qu'elle n'est qu'un malentendu.

Je ne suis point le martyr et le souffrant que vous aimez tant à peindre ; je suis simplement un homme qui travaille avec conviction à sa modeste tâche et qui trouve pleine satisfaction dans ce travail. Si parfois j'ai dû passer pour cela quelque temps en prison, eh bien ! je m'y suis reposé de mes fatigues physiques, sans ressentir de très grandes incommodités, pour ne pas parler de souffrances.

Du point de vue de votre mentalité, vous devriez au fond désirer que j'aille plus souvent en prison et que j'y reste le plus longtemps possible. Mais lorsque vous protestez contre cela, votre conduite, passez-moi cette vérité, me faire rire.

Car nous sommes des ennemis, et des ennemis irréductibles, j'en suis sûr. L'écrivain honnête est toujours ennemi de la société actuelle, à plus forte raison ennemi de ceux qui défendent et justifient l'âpreté au gain et l'esprit de domination, ces bases fondamentales de l'organisation sociale d'aujourd'hui.

Vous dites encore : « Nous aimons Gorki, et lui... »

Messieurs ! Je vous le dis très sincèrement : votre amour de bourgeois n'est pour moi, socialiste, qu'une profonde offense !

J'espère que ces lignes détermineront exactement et pour toujours nos rapports réciproques.

Maxime Gorki.

The Sormovo factory worker, Peter Zalamov, and his mother, the

On the other hand, the summer which Gorky spent in the United States at the Martin's cottage in the Adironacks was a creatively fruitful period. It was then that he wrote his characteristically proletarian work *The Mother* and the play *Enemies,* besides a series of extremely violent political pamphlets, *In America* and *My Interviews.* Gorky revealed himself as a powerful but rude pamphleteer. The bitter sarcasm with which he branded American capitalism, German militarism, and the cupidity of French finance in these imaginary interviews is very likely unsurpassed. But bitter or sweet, he was unaware of the subtle art of irony.

prototypes of the protagonists of *The Mother:* Paul Vlassov and Nilovna.

In *The Mother,* the writer was inspired by real events which had taken place, as we have already mentioned, in the factories at Sormovo. He had known its heroes: the worker Zalomov (Paul Vlassov in the story) was awakened intellectually and had become involved in revolutionary activity; his mother Anna (Nilovna) an illiterate yet shrewd peasant, had volunteered for the dangerous mission of distributing pamphlets. Back in Nizhni in October, 1902, shortly before the workers' trial, Gorky had taken an active part in the organization of their defense.

Appearing in an American magazine in 1906, then in book

form in New York and London, the novel saw a Russian language printing only in Berlin. The labor press in the West took it up at once, principally in Germany, followed by France and Italy, and it was circulated by the million either as *feuilletons* or daily supplements. In Russia, only the first part, heavily censored, was allowed to appear in 1907, in the *Znaniye Miscellanies,* and this was soon seized. The Press Bureau decided to sue the author "on the charge of disseminating a work which incites the commission of grave offenses, provokes the hostility of the workers towards the propertied classes, and calls to riot and acts of rebellion."

But if the uncut version of *The Mother* was not to be printed legally in Russia until after 1917, secretly the Berlin Russian language edition had a huge circulation.

The play, *Enemies,* written around the same time as *The Mother*, was inspired with the same proletarian feelings. It, too, was prohibited.

Final scene of *Enemies*, Moscow Art Theater.

It may be noted that in the files of the Russian police this world-famous writer who evoked great waves of passion, love, and hate on both sides of the Atlantic was still called Alexei Peshkov, "son of Maxim, an artisan of the Nizhni Novgorod house-painters' guild."

On his return from America in the autumn of 1906, Gorky sought a refuge. After the commotion of his propaganda against the loan to the Czar, any re-entry into Russia was out of the question. In October he settled down on Capri, where he was to stay for seven years.

We must imagine the special atmosphere of this residence. If ever there were two contradictory and irreconcilable notions in the world they were surely "Capri" and "Gorky," the meeting of the enchanted isle, "mother of Latin games and Greek delights," and this coarse son of the Volga. For the seven years that Gorky was to spend on Capri, just as for his later years in Sorrento, or his years in Germany, or his summer in America and Paris, he carried with him the whole of Russia, blind and invulnerable to the surrounding world. Living a good part of his life abroad, he was never to learn one word of a foreign language. No foreign landscape caught his eye, his works are devoid of any imprint. His brief and colorless *Tales of Italy* possess nothing Italian except for some superficial embellishments of local color as conventional as his "city-planner" descriptions of New York. Moreover in a preface Gorky explained that although they were sketches of real events, he called them "tales" because nature and life in Italy bore so slight a resemblance to the Russian; and for him only Russia stood for reality. In Germany, in America, or in Italy, he continued to deal with his one and only subject, the special destiny of the Russian man, and to describe his unique landscape – the vast and melancholy Russian terrains – without regard for the waters of the Tyrrhenian Sea and the blue grottoes. It was on Capri that he thought up one of his most significant pieces, *Okurov Town* (1910), a caricature of petty-bourgeois stagnation in the Russian province. Amid all the charms of Capri his homesickness knew no limits. "If a tooth could feel after being knocked out, it would probably feel as lonely as I did," is what he wrote concerning his nostalgia. With all the more eagerness did he welcome everything that arrived from Russia.

Many malicious rumors grew out of this residence at Capri, concerning the "gilded cage" in which his mistress, Madame Andreyeva held prisoner this writer of the proletariat. But it was true that Marie Fiodorovna Andreyeva, rich and generous, devoted herself to enveloping in comfort this sickly and tireless worker who was her companion. She was hardly an ordinary woman. A long-time actress with the Art Theater, she had years before left her husband, a general, in order to devote herself to revolutionary activities. It was with full awareness

Capri, 1908.

that she followed Gorky, not only as a woman but also as a comrade-in-arms. Besides, Gorky had at his disposal from then on his own impressive income from royalties – for repeated reprintings of his works in Russia, translations into every language, and productions in theaters everywhere. His fame was tremendous. Modest and unselfish, he had as it were no personal needs. The main item on his budget besides books was aid to the party treasury and to countless petitioners. He often intervened or lent money without having been asked, simply because he had sensed desperation in spite of the restraint of a correspondent's letter.

By now the number of these correspondents was almost incalculable. Capri became a second Ysnaya Polyana to which from all corners of Russia flowed the questions, the sufferings, the dreams of men. These men were very different from the types who, preoccupied with self-perfection, sought the well-being of their souls at the side of the great abstemious and vegetarian moralist, the enemy of modern civilization. Gorky was a "bad teacher," a teacher who preached the joy of living, the triumph of culture, the struggle against misery.

Tolstoy used to appear only briefly in his court of followers, dangling before them some word which they solemnly received. Most of the time he enjoyed the protective barrier that the Countess threw up around him in order to defend the work of the genius against unimportant intruders, drawing upon herself the displeasure of the Tolstoyans. Gorky, on the contrary, spent his life within reach of everyone. Nothing – not even his writing, which he always appraised with extreme modesty – seemed to him as precious as the contact with the humblest human being. Naturally, on Capri visitors were more rare, although when we consider the distance from Russia their number was surprising. Any Russian going to Italy looked on it as his duty to make this pilgrimage, not to mention those who were invited by Gorky and Madame Andreyeva to spend several days or months; friends, invalids, starving, desperate people whom they set back on their feet or whom they dosed with the cure of optimism.

But most of all there were the letters, an enormous correspondence which poured in from the heart of Russia. Crude letters bearing unlikely addresses, "Switzerland. Isle of Cyprus. Gorky," they arrived somehow, the confessions, the manuscripts, and the endless questions. He read every letter seriously, attentively, and answered them all. He was perhaps the only great writer who took care that no humble person was hurt by his hand.

THE CALL OF FAITH

From the time of Gorky's entry onto the world scene, his life was marked by outbursts, loud demonstrations, and even scandals. He was always in the spotlight. But deep within him, running parallel to this spectacular movement, his spiritual life maintained its course, filled with the call of faith, an unseen but constant stream revealing itself at times in telltale ripples, bursting forth one day in the violent whirlpool of a religious crisis.

This religious sentiment had its beginning in the primitive, radiant belief breathed into the boy by his grandmother, an illiterate peasant possessing a splendid gift of poetry. The writer devoted to her some of the most beautiful pages of his masterpiece, *My Childhood.*

Grandmother lived with God in trusting intimacy; she was "on good terms with Him." "Her God was with her all day," wrote Gorky. "She even spoke to the animals about Him." He was the God of inner happiness. Just the opposite was "Grandfather's God, a severe judge.... He put no trust in man, He always insisted on penance, and He loved to chastise."

> In those days my thoughts and feelings about God were the chief nourishment of my soul and the most beautiful of my existence.... God was the best and brightest of all the

beings who lived about me – grandmother's God, that Dear Friend of all creation. . . . My childish distinction between the two Gods troubled and divided my soul.

Very early, the boy took to the atmosphere of the church: "Whatever the priest or the deacon recited – that was to grandfather's God; but the choir always sang to grandmother's God." He arranged his own little nook in a pit in the garden and set the inside with bits of colored glass and broken pieces of china; ". . . when the sun looked into the pit they all shone with a rainbow effect, like one sees in churches." For in his sordid, miserable life, the most beautiful thing he knew was the church.

Later, in 1907, when Gorky was in London as a delegate to the Fifth Congress of the Bolshevik faction of the Social Democratic party, he was to describe with distaste the Presbyterian church which housed the meetings; "absurdly unadorned, resembling a classroom in a poor school."

At the age of fourteen, Alexei worked for an icon merchant, and then as a "god-dauber" in the studio. There the strange world of self-taught theologians, Old Believers, and religious sects opened up to him. He quickly placed them on the side of "Grandfather's God," severe and intractable. Yet the determination of these tormented nonconformists, the fiercely poetic glow enveloping them, made a profound impression on him, and more than once he was to return to them, infusing the veins of his characters with the untamed blood of these men who courageously resisted the offical authorities.

At the age of twenty-three, Gorky set off on foot across Russia. In the Kuban region, he was accidentally implicated in a Cossack mutiny and apprehended. What should they find in his knapsack but a Gospel which, he said, "was very compromising."

As a young writer he did not seem plagued by religious questions. Only from time to time did a word betray the presence of this submerged current. "People are fools," he wrote to Chekhov in 1900. "In order to make their lives easier, they would need God. Yet they reject and ridicule those who affirm Him." Then after referring to Soloviov and d'Annunzio, he reverted suddenly to his original thought, "Is God necessary, what do you think, Anton Pavlovitch?"

After his first visit to Tolstoy, overwhelmed by the powerful figure of the man, he wrote similarly to Chekhov:

Until then I couldn't imagine that Tolstoy was an atheist, although I had sensed it, but on listening to him speak of Christ and on seeing his eyes, too shrewd for a believer, I knew that he was truly and deeply an atheist. That's so, isn't it?

For his part, "the old sorcerer" as Gorky called him, sounded out the young writer, "And suddenly he asked me, exactly as if he were dealing me a blow":

"Why don't you believe in God?"

"I have no faith, Leo Nikolaevitch."

"It is not true. . . . You will realize it one day. Your disbelief comes from obstinacy, from shyness: the world is not

With Tolstoy, 1901.

what you would like it to be. Now, you love much, and faith is only a greater love. A non-believer cannot love. By nature you are a believer and you can not get on without God."

Even after 1928, the year marking his total adherence to the ideological platform of the Soviets, Gorky, in order to convey the sublime, made use of the categories of the divine and the sacred. To glorify work, he spoke of its "you might say religious meaning." Or else, in praising the works of men, he was to say to his working-class audience, "Let me express it by a word in disgrace these days: I respect them and venerate them as holy."

For a long time the religious theme was to remain present in Gorky without crystallizing. For example, the drama of the hero in his second novel, *Three of Them* (1910): Ilia Luniev, a restless and tormented boy, had in his veins the tumultuous blood of the Old Believers. He was troubled by a vague faith; he liked the atmosphere of the church, which he attended regularly. Taken with a prostitute, he killed the old moneylender who was supplying her with funds. (The theme and certain developments are comparable to *Crime and Punishment.*) Without its being expressly shown, the turbulence which brought him to confess his crime was of a religious essence.

The big crisis burst forth in *The Confession* (1908).

Once settled down in the peace and quiet of Capri, Gorky collected himself, and the preoccupations of his inner life seethed with all the more force, just as in the far-off country towards which his whole being was turned, religious thought was enjoying an irresistible revival. The failure of the revolution of 1905, followed by a cruel repression, deeply demoralized the liberal intelligentsia; abandoning materialism and action, it sought an escape in religious philosophy. This was the period of the "turning inward" of the revolution, raised to the spiritual level, become the personal affair of every individual.

The Left deceived itself no more than the Right. The activists interpreted this new profession of faith as a betrayal of the revolutionary cause on the part of the elite of the intelligentsia, while reactionary circles welcomed it with satisfaction.

A certain group formed at the turn of the century, under the name of "seekers after God," did its utmost to harmonize the revolution and religion. At first, it had been linked with Symbolism, in particular with the scant but weighty poetic work of the religious philosopher, Vladimir Soloviov (whom Gorky had read very attentively). Soon a split developed, and the "radicals" set themselves a new task. They wanted to spiritualize Marxism. Thus was born a doctrine no longer of "seeking" but of "building" God.

The difference between the two tendencies hinged on their concepts of God. The "seekers" remained basically faithful to traditional Christianity: their quest was for a Third Testament. For the "builders," God did not yet exist, but the collective effort of humanity was to build a God, eminently social and socialistic. This theory, which received its outstanding formulation in Bogdanov's system (he was a former comrade of Lenin), lured other prominent Marxists, such as Lunacharsky, Bazarov, Pokrovsky, etc. It was to this group that Maxim Gorky devoted himself passionately.

He was all the more easily enticed by Bogdanovism because its philosophical and political aspects escaped him. Gorky stated repeatedly that he was not a political person and that he understood nothing of philosophical theories. He was unable to follow Lenin's thinking as the latter condemned Bogdanovism philosophically, for its "deviation" from Marxism (inspired by Mach); and politically, for its adoption of simplistic tactics at odds with his own strategy.

Gorky's socialism never went beyond a primitive level – love of man, confidence in man – not unlike his Christianity. This made him all the more receptive to the social aspect of Bogdanov's idealism. Self-taught, he had a passion for reason, he expected good to come from it alone, and he was unable to accept the fundamental Marxist formula which holds that "it is not the consciousness of men which determines their existence," but on the contrary "their social existence which determines their consciousness." Gorky's whole personal struggle was one of overcoming his own "social condition" through the help of his "consciousness"!

Besides, Bogdanov was infinitely closer to Gorky in his belief (as distinguished from Marx's) that "the social was inseparable from moral consciousness," and likewise, in his conception of progress as "the fullness and the harmony growing out of the exercise of moral consciousness." This was presented as "the organizing principle of social practice," the economics being only "an adjunct to technological and ideological development." Aspiring, like Marx, to a society without classes, Bogdanov felt that it would be attained not in transferring the instruments of production to the workers, but in re-educating the working class by means of "proletarian culture." This re-education, this transition from the economic to the ideologic, corresponded to Gorky's ideas. He, too, would "give to the proletariat a coherent and unified education, which would unalterably determine the collective will and mentality" as opposed to bourgeois individualism. That "unalterable unity" of the proletariat would at last make it possible "that they set out to build a new life, in universal harmony and brotherhood."

These ideas lent themselves easily to popularization, and endowed Gorky's primitive idealism with charm. What he did with these ideas we see in *The Confession,* a novel published in 1908 and dedicated to Chaliapin, his intimate friend. It is a valuable document of the struggle unleashed in the soul of a man who wanted to be both a Marxist and a Christian. In this theme lay its starkly realistic fascination.

Let us not be put off by its somewhat monotonous form; Gorky had conceived of it as a didactic work which he wanted to call "the life of a saint *or something of that sort.*" He gave free rein to his compassionate disposition, his talent for marvelous descriptions of nature and for lyric phrasing. It is a sort of long prose poem (168 pages) into which has stolen, here and there, "that blasted rhythmic prose," one of the writer's forgivable sins.

A man tells the story of his life: a foundling born "in the weeds," having known hunger from his first day. Taken in by a sexton, Larion – "a very strange and lonely man," "a tender and gentle soul," with a passion for animals and beloved of them, who sang the liturgical chants like an angel – the child spent whole magic days with him in church or in the forest. (A good many of the motifs recall *My Childhood,* which was not to be written until six years later.) But life was exceedingly difficult and the boy was soon to ask the question, "Why does God help man so little?"

Tormented by this fundamental question, Matvei went out into the world in search of God. He spent two years in a monastery, consulted hermits and monks reputed to be saints, became a pilgrim, and yet found no answer to his anxious question. Before man's suffering "his faith in the omniscience of God and the justice of his law cracks," until the day when, on the edge of a wood, he meets a little old man, a gay and spritely wanderer who *knew.* By one of those symbols which reveal an author's design, Gorky bestowed on him the name Jehudiil (which had been his own pen-name at the time of his debut in journalism).

Jehudiil affirmed nothing, nor did he pretend to possess the truth. He only taught Matvei that God was still to be created; and that the "builders," who were none other than the factory workers, were devoted to his creation. So it was to the factory, a new type of mecca, that Matvei-Gorky, the seeker, was sent by Jehudiil-Gorky, the finder. Among the alert workers, reading their books, absorbing their wisdom, the seeker was to discover the true path towards God. But he and his new friends were hunted by the police and, seeker-turned-builder, Matvei left the factory to carry the good word to the masses.

"The last blow, the blow which finished the construction of the temple" was delivered to his soul by a miracle: In front of the entrance to a convent, a young paralyzed girl was lying, inert, on a stretcher. A procession of religious pilgrims drew near. Seized by the excitement of the frenzied crowd, wafted upward by its breath, by the mysterious power of the divine and popular emanations, the paralytic got up and began to walk.

Such was the latest work of the author who one year before had written *The Mother*. Yet perhaps even in that book, insufficient emphasis has been put on certain passages which were hardly lacking in faith. Hastily written, conforming to a specific "social demand," it remains the sole "proletarian" work in the author's enormous output. Nevertheless, as preoccupied as they were with direct action, his characters did not forget God. In a curious conversation, one of the revolutionaries said: "Christ was not strong in spirit. 'Let the cup pass from me,' he said. And he recognized Caesar. God cannot recognize human powers. He himself is the whole power. He does not divide his soul saying: so much for the godly, so much for the human. . . ."

On the other hand, one person stands out, warm and radiant among the "model" characters; Nilovna, "the mother," having discovered a new humanity, also discovered a new God: "Christ would not have been, either, if men hadn't perished for his sake."

Очень и очень рад,
что Бог помогает
театру. Трудно
нам с ней бороться —
— и внутренние
военные и финансо-
вые трудности необы-
чайны — а все же
пока живы.

Немирович

P.S. А Современник
подгадил так и
впереди! Хороший по-
дарок к его дорого

LENIN VERSUS GORKY: THE RELIGIOUS CONFLICT

Gorky's "deviation" exasperated Lenin. It went far beyond the mere publication of a novel. Thanks to Gorky, Capri had become the cradle of Bogdanovist dissidence. Under the political reaction which was raging in Russia, the activity of secret groups and the training of leaders had become increasingly difficult. Among the Social-Democratic emigrés there was a preoccupation with the establishment of a school for revolutionary propagandists in some other country, where selected workers could be brought from Russia. Gorky had offered his villa on Capri for this purpose.

Soon the students began to arrive, after having secretly crossed the Russian frontier. The curriculum was extensive, the greater part allotted to Bolshevik theoreticians. Gorky's conference notes on the history of Russian literature, which he presented as the development of revolutionary ideas, are extant.

In the summer of 1907, Lenin came to Capri to prepare for the opening of the institution. But when the school got under way (in the summer of 1909 there were twenty students) and he discovered its "deviationist" tendencies, he circulated a resolution in his *Proletariat* (published in Paris) stating that "the Bolshevik faction of the party cannot assume responsibility for the Capri school." He himself refused to teach courses there, and set up his own school at Longjumeau,

Page of a letter from Lenin to Gorky.

drawing to it a group of Capri students. The Capri institution underwent some internal differences and then went out of existence. Yet Lenin's anger was understandable. Of course, he knew that Gorky had never tried to convert the school into an instrument for splitting the party. He knew Gorky to be too honest (and no doubt too naive) to fear any political maneuver on his part. But he was shrewd enough not to minimize the extent of his "deviation," nor to fail to understand that with Gorky it was not a passing whim but a matter of faith, deep and ineradicable; a faith that Lenin considered a menace to the work of the revolution. However, he was also aware of just how much the writer's talent served the cause of the revolution, and he held himself in check.

> I understand, my dear Alexei Maximovitch, how depressed you must feel. You have chanced to get a glimpse of the labor movement and social-democracy from an angle, in such manifestations and forms, as have more than once in the history of Russia and western Europe reduced intellectual skeptics to despair concerning the labor movement and social-democracy. I am certain that this will not happen to you, and I should like to grasp your hand firmly. With your artistic gift you have so tremendously benefited the labor movement in Russia – and not only in Russia – and you will so much benefit it in the future, that it is inadmissable for you to fall under oppressive moods as a result of episodes (among our quarreling emigrés) of our "campaign abroad."

This conflict with Lenin was all the more painful for Gorky who, by his own avowal, had "loved this man as no other." But the two were separated by temperament, intellect, and also upbringing. Lenin, a lawyer, born into the petty gentry, the son of a secondary-school director, was prepared by disposition as well as by education for methodical studies. He was dominated by an inflexible logic when he recognized the soundness of some line of reasoning, and set against any concession or half-measures. A complete materialist, he approached any problem, and particularly the religious problem, strictly from the political and social angle.

Gorky, an artist, a subjective person, had emerged from the very depths of the common people, from an illiterate background. Several months spent in a parish school was all he had of academic training. Self-taught, he owed his vast but disorganized knowledge to his enormous reading. He had made an ideal of his thirst for knowledge; he had sworn a genuine worship of learning, and upheld a primitive, popular religiosity, an intuitive, and therefore all the more powerful, Christianity.

Lenin implored Gorky for more pieces "like *The Mother*." He would not have Gorky distracted with requests that he "waste himself on newspaper articles," and begrudged Gorky even more the "waste" of energy and time that *The Confession* had cost. But most of all, he attacked the writer's followers, whom he accused of "wishing to profit (ideologically) from Gorky's enormous prestige, thereby preserving and using his weaknesses, which are precisely the negative element in the great amount of good that he has brought to the proletariat."

Although Lenin restrained himself in regard to Gorky at the time of the publication of the novel, the conflict erupted violently several years later. In 1913, Gorky published in a Moscow newspaper a violent diatribe against the "corrupting" spirit of Dostoevsky. His attitude was warmly applauded by Lenin. But an unfortunate sentence escaped the writer: "As for the quest after God, it must be set aside for a while."

For a while! In this one expression, Lenin saw a definite sign of what was happening in the back of Gorky's mind.

> It follows that you are against *bogoiskatelstvo* [god-seeking] only "for a while"!! It follows that you are against *bogoiskatelstvo* only in order to replace it by *bogostroitelstvo* [god-building]!! Now isn't it terrible that such a thing should *follow* from your words? God-seeking differs from god-building or god-creating not a whit more than a yellow devil differs from a blue devil. . . .

And the violent, unyielding invective continued at great length, to conclude: "Searching through your article, and *probing* how such a *slip* could have cropped forth, I am at a loss. What is it? The residue of *The Confession*, of which you *yourself* disapproved? Its echo?"

It was not a slip, and Lenin knew it, for several days later he wrote to Gorky once again:

> In the matter of god, the divine, and everything connected with it, you are contradicting yourself. . . . You have broken

(or seemingly broken) with [the Bogdanovists] without having grasped the ideologic bases of their doctrine. Similarly, now, you are "vexed", you write that you are "unable to understand how the expression 'for a while' slipped out" – and at the same time you continue to defend the idea of god and god-building.

And to clarify his point that, in short, Gorky was only repeating the "hocus-pocus of priestery":

> The idea of god is divested of its *historic* and *actual* substance (filth, prejudices, the sanction of darkness and wretchedness, on the one side, and of feudal bondage and the monarchy, on the other), and in place of this reality is inserted a goody-goody philistine phrase (God: "ideas which awaken and organize social feelings."). By that you mean "the good," you intend a reference to "Truth-Justice," etc. This noble intention is yours personally, a subjective "innocent desire." But the minute you put it in writing, this "good" was carried to the *masses,* and its significance is no longer determined by your noble intention, but by the relation of social forces, the objective correlation of classes. By virtue of this correlation it follows (despite your will, and regardless of your thought) that you have colored and sugared the idea of the priesthood (of the extreme right) and Nicholas II because *in reality* the idea of god helps *them* to keep the people in bondage. By having prettified the idea of god, you have prettified the chains by which they bind the ignorant workers and *muzhiks.*

Even while rejecting the constituted church – whose God was, for him, "Grandfather's" – and having completely accepted party doctrine, Gorky nevertheless continued until the end of his days to dream of a synthesis of socialism and faith:

> For the proletariat, the time has passed when faith and knowledge were as inimical as falsehood and truth. Where the proletariat rules and everything is created by its mighty hand, there is no room for dissension between knowledge and faith; faith is the product of man's knowledge of the power of reason, and this faith, while it creates heroes, does not create, and will not create, gods. . . .

Unless – and here we see again the "builder" – unless "God be created in the image of Man."

Gorky wrote that Alexander Blok, the poet, told him one day that he was glad to note that in Gorky the proletarian writer was not monopolized solely by social problems. "I have always felt that this is not your real self," he said, "but that you are worried by 'childish questions' – the most deep and terrible of all."

"Blok," added Gorky, "was mistaken." No, the perceptive poet was not mistaken: All his life Maxim Gorky remained troubled by great "childish" questions.

ANTI-DOSTOEVSKY

The "slip" which had given Gorky away occurred in a letter to the editor published, in September, 1913, in a widely distributed Moscow newspaper, protesting the Art Theater's intention of producing *The Possessed.* In the name of ethics, and above all civic spirit, Gorky stormed against the power of suggestion that a stage version would confer on Dostoevsky's morbid characters. The recent adaptation of *The Brothers Karamazov* had made a profound impression on the spectators, and had contributed to aggravating the depressed atmosphere of those years when, on the eve of war, Russian society had slipped "into the void."

Gorky's grievances against Dostoevsky were of an emotional – one might even say impassioned – nature. What was involved was no mere expression of antipathy or reproach, but a sort of "squaring of accounts." Gorky fought against Dostoevsky in the name of that which he cherished as most sacred. And yet the shadow of the "cruel genius" was present in his own work; haunted by certain Dostoevskyan themes, he took the opposite tack with that much more vehemence. Moreover, all Russian literature of the end of the nineteenth and the beginning of the twentieth centuries was floundering within the infernal circle that this sorcerer's apprentice had drawn. Gorky borrowed from him certain themes, certain situations; but he simplified them, stripping them of their voodoo power, their morbid relish that is the very core of Dostoevsky's genius.

Russian criticism had been quick to notice that Gorky was dependent on him for several things: a way of introducing the narrator's "I," a way of approaching urban themes, and of presenting the inner life of his characters. Many passages of *The Spy* or *Okurov Town* showed this influence, not to mention *Three of Them* in which, as we have indicated, there is a compelling parallel between the murder of the old money-changer by Luniev and the murder of the old money-lender by Raskolnikov.

Still, haunted by the author of *The Brothers Karamazov*, Gorky kept up his revolt against him. His first acquaintance with Dostoevsky's writing dated from the 1880's, and within a quarter of a century, on Capri, he had re-read him entirely. Not without naivety, he said: "Although overwhelming in beauty, certain things in him remained strange to me. For a long time now I have been unable to understand why the student Raskolnikov killed the old woman, and why a Frenchman, Paul Bourget's *Disciple*, felt the need to imitate the Russian student."

Some years back, Soviet criticism made no secret of the Gorky-Dostoevsky affinity-hostility. But since the strict tightening up after the last war, the critics seem to have been vigorously called to order: Gorky is not to be taxed with any suggestion of a link to Dostoevsky, the despicable class enemy, relentlessly condemned and purged from Russian libraries. The critics, including the dramatic critics, were encouraged to admit their error, on the occasion of the production of Gorky's *The Old Man* in 1946, when they said that the main character of the play, with his "essential blend of villainy and nobility, intellectualism and depravity, was characteristic of the *Karamozovian Soul*."

However, Soviet criticism before 1946 had shed interesting light on the sociological aspect of the choice of heroes common to the two writers. Both were singers of the fallen man. But while Dostoevsky's hero was a noble, a functionary, or a landlord who had fallen, Gorky's hero was rising. He was the *déclassé* peasant or artisan, who had nothing to lose. Both were victims caught in the turmoil of new-born capitalism. But if Dostoevsky's hero lived the general social tragedy through his own individual tragedy, Gorky's man had everything to gain in enclosing himself in collectivity, within the frame of the rising proletarian class.

At present – to judge from writings to the end of 1953 – official Soviet doctrine would have it that from the very first, Gorky, rather than being subject to the influence of Dostoevsky, had deliberately *parodied* him; thus we have the murder committed by Luniev, the character of Luka, the "false consoler" of *The Lower Depths,* and so on. Soviet criticism would like to assign Dostoevsky to the West (or at least to the Russian emigrés), carrying this to the point of establishing a direct link between *Crime and Punishment* and . . . Charlie Chaplin's *Monsieur Verdoux!* Gorky himself set the tone when he wrote in a letter in 1933:

> It is his [Dostoevsky's] "philosophy" on which the current political reaction feeds, in orienting itself towards individualism and nihilism; that is what the "internal enemies" of democracy lean on. The time has come to attack Dostoevskyism all along the line.

And farther on: "I should prefer that the civilized world were unified not by Dostoevsky but by Pushkin, for the tremendous, universal genius of Pushkin is a psychically healthy and purifying genius."

Whenever Gorky wanted to define the ways of literature, he did so by using Dostoevsky as a foil. Thus, in his report to the First Congress of Soviet Writers (1934) condemning meta-

physical absolutism, departure from realism, and social bankruptcy, he represented Dostoevskyism not only as an undoubted evil, but as the "supreme evil." In his notes toward a manual of literature for the use of young writers, in proposing to them a new type of hero, Gorky warned against Dostoevsky who, he said, always left in his heroes an unconscious side, never quite tracing them back to their social origins. Now, that is exactly what Gorky himself neglected to do, and the few times he forced himself to draw not men, but class products, he failed. For the proletarian class, we have the example of the schematic, lifeless figure of Vlassov in *The Mother*, and for the intellectual class, we have Klim Samgin, obviously a puppet. On the contrary, where his characters were successful, where they were convincing, like Konovalov, Paul Goremyka, Foma, or their numerous brothers, they were suffused in a dense and troubled atmosphere, beyond the grip of class determinism. None of Gorky's memorable characters are simple, although alongside Dostoevsky's their conflicts and torments seem so.

Gorky drew directly on Dostoevsky for two human types particularly dear to Russian literature, the "sainted prostitute" and the "intellectual."

With the exception of his first romantic heroines, Izergil and Malva, who were in a way female bossiaks, Gorky's women were two-sided beings. Thrown into lives of debauchery, they concealed the souls of mothers and saints. There was Medinskaia, the village coquette who, after having made game of Foma Gordeiev, confessed to him that, confronted by the impurity of her life, her soul "is split into judge and criminal"; she sent the young man off in order not to hurt him. Another woman of loose morals, attracted to him, taught him about the world and, in the face of his basic purity, left him in order not to be a burden on his life. Then Sasha, the mysterious débauchée with a sad, hypnotic voice, who knew herself to be pure, cried to Foma: "Don't you dare mention my soul! It is none of your business! I'm the only one who may speak of it! . . . When the time comes I, too, will begin to think. . . . That will be the finish of me. . . ."

Noble, unselfish, and tragic, these women fill the pages of Gorky's writings, reaching their height in Vera, the prostitute of *Three of Them*, who, rather than bare her soul in front of the jury, preferred to let herself be convicted. Over all of these women, hovers the shadow of Sonia Marmiladova *(Crime and Punishment)*, or Nastasia Filipovna (*The Idiot*).

With regard to the Dostoevskyian man, Gorky's position was more complex. Fascinated by his subtlety, he rejected it; admiring his intellectualism, he decided to combat it. In vengeance against the consuming grip of the concept, he reduced Dostoevskyian man to the level of a "petty bourgeois," thereby charging its author with the gravest offense in the scale of Russian values.

The expression "petty bourgeois" is one of the key terms of Russian intellectual life. Since the beginning of democratic literature in the middle of the nineteenth century, all men of letters, indeed all intellectuals, employed it constantly with every nuance of scorn, applying it to philistines, pedants, smug people, and those without intelligence. In his *Notes on the Petty Bourgeois Mentality*, Gorky stretched the social sense of this insult to cover the intellectuals who pretended to hold the monopoly on intelligence. Between the two battling camps, he said, that of the aristocrats defending their power and that of the slaves aspiring to liberation,

> the petty bourgeois would like to live in calm and beauty, without participating in this struggle, their favorite situation being a peaceful existence behind the stronger army.... They always seek to retard the normal development of class contradictions ... to reconcile the irreconcilable ...

and reap the reward of a typically petty-bourgeois malady, " 'pangs of conscience,' another form of their 'humanism.' " Tossing between two camps,

> the petty bourgeois are ashamed to go to the right, and they are afraid to go to the left.... Therefore, they hide as well as they can in the obscure folds of mysticism, in the charming bowers of estheticism ... in metaphysical labyrinths, in order to return to the narrow roads of religion, cluttered with the bric-a-brac of a secular falsehood....

The ugliest trait of the petty borgeois was their attitude towards the people; they glorified its sufferings the better to enjoy the fruits of its labor. In a famous polemic, Gorky cast the blame on Russian literature, which dealt with nothing but a people eternally resigned, to whom Dostoevsky cried, "Endure!" and Tolstoy, "Do not resist evil with violence!" And he concluded, "This is a monstrous thing!"

Gorky knew very well that the storm aroused by his *Notes* had nothing to do with his condemnation of philistinism, which no one in Russia would have dared to defend anyway. His heresy lay in ascribing philistinism to Tolstoy and Dostoevsky! But he had the staunch support of Lenin who appreciated the tremendous social import of the *Notes*.

The picture became complicated when Gorky admitted that "conscience" drove certain intellectuals "to go to the people." But then, either they limited themselves to spreading the alphabet without realizing the revolutionary consequences, or they practiced Tolstoyan "self-perfection," "pitiful burlesque," or else, "they went to the revolution in the style of English sportsmen who travel from London to the Caspian in order to hunt wild ducks," free to change their minds according to "their capricious whim."

Having reduced Dostoevsky's man to the level of the petty bourgeois by identifying him with the intellectual, Gorky was to hold on to this theme. *Notes* was followed by *The Destruction of the Person* (1909), in which the same epithets occurred, with the addition of a tirade against those writers who were partisans of "art for art's sake," attacking their eroticism, estheticism, and "decadence."

Through every portrait of an intellectual that Gorky chose to paint, one can see the outline of the Stavrogins and the Karamazovs. Gorky gives the explanation through the mouth of Karamora (story by that name, 1924). A revolutionary turned *agent provocateur,* in prison, knowing that he is going to die, Karamora wrote his confession.

> One feels as one writes how much cleverer and better one becomes. It is an intoxicating job. It makes one understand Dostoevsky. He was a writer particularly inclined to intoxicate himself with the mad, stormy, irrational game of his imagination, a game which consisted of feeling many people within himself.

The figure of the intellectual in Gorky's work was to undergo a certain evolution, starting with the journalist Iejov (in *Foma Gordeiev*, 1898), a fallen man but sincerely idealistic, continuing up to Klim Samgin, the caricature of an entire class. Essentially egocentric, these heroes of Gorky ceased to be alive, but became contrivances. Indeed, Chekhov had sent him a warning: "In the delineation of the intelligentsia there is something forced, as if you feel a sense of uncertainty. This is not due to a lack of study of the intelligentsia; you know them, but it seems as if you do not know from what angle to approach them." All his life, Gorky retained this lack of assurance regarding the intelligentsia. A quarter of a century later he confessed: "I feel myself completely powerless to draw in words the figures of the short-sighted bookworms in pince-nez or spectacles, in 'blousing' trousers, in varied waistcoats and monotonously speckled cloaks of learned words."

Aware of his weakness in painting this class, the creator of such intensely alive tramps and common people found himself an excuse in passing off as a literary method that which was really a defect: these characters lack life, he said, because their originals do. "I am now writing," he informed Stefan Zweig in a letter on March 15, 1925, "a book about Russian men who, more than any others, know how to invent their lives and to invent themselves. . . ." According to the author, the word "invent" was to be the key to Klim and others like him, who posed as misunderstood superior men; desperately empty, they did no more than appropriate the intelligence of others, debasing everything they touched. They knew only the pose and the phraseology of revolutionary *élan*.

> I wanted to depict in Samgin an intellectual of "medium worth;" he goes through a whole series of states of mind seeking for himself an independent place where he will be comfortable, materially and in his inner life . . . in the guise of "a spiritual aristocrat." Klim was a revolutionary in spite of himself, out of fear of the inevitable revolution, and felt himself the victim of history.

Gorky conceived of *The Life of Klim Samgin* as a vast, historic fresco extending over the forty years which preceded the revolution of 1917. *Klim* was to be the crowning of his work. We find in it numerous stories, people, and episodes recorded by the writer during his long career. But they had lost all vitality, because they were seen through human beings who were "invented and who invent themselves." This novel was a real *Bouvard and Pécuchet* * of the intelligentsia. But two thousand pages of Bouvard and Pécuchet!

Eternally fascinated by these lusterless, mechanically complex heroes, it was to them that the writer dedicated the artistic activity of his last twelve years, painting with passion, despair, and impotence this intelligentsia that he so painfully loved and which had so bitterly disappointed him. This attachment, which was the great drama of Gorky's life, formed the basis of the second conflict with Lenin.

---

* *Bouvard and Pécuchet,* a satirical novel by Flaubert, is about two men in their middle years who set out to improve themselves. (Trans. note.)

"Maxim Gorky has come back to Russia!"
Russian cartoon, 1914.

GORKY VERSUS LENIN: THE CONFLICT OVER THE INTELLIGENTSIA

At the end of 1913, urged on by Lenin and reassured by Chaliapin, a court favorite, Gorky decided to take advantage of the amnesty accorded on the occasion of the 300th anniversary of Romanov power, and he returned to Russia. The court action had been shelved, but the police department at once ordered a 24-hour "shadow" on the writer.

The war split the Social Democratic and Social Revolutionary parties down the middle. Some, Plekhanov, Kropotkin, Deutsch, Vera Zasulitch, declared themselves in favor of the war against German militarism; they were termed "social patriots" by Lenin, Zinoviev, and Bukharin who, themselves, preferred "defeatism," hoping that defeat of the Russian Empire would result in revolution. Gorky, by nature opposed to all war, sided with the Leninists with such enthusiasm that he readily turned his back on Zinovi Peshkov, his adopted son, who fought in the ranks of the French army (he is a general now, and a French ambassador).

Under the iron-bound conditions of military censorship, Gorky, resorting frequently to "that cursed allegorical Aesopian language," waged a desperate fight against the right-wing bourgeoisie, capitalism, colonialism ("the white menace"), anti-Semitism, in other words, against oppression in all its forms. He managed to give a defeatist tone to the magazine, *Chronicles* (*Letopis*), which he founded in 1915. In 1914, he published the first *Anthology of Proletarian Writers* (the second appeared in 1917), which marked an important step towards a really democratic literature.

However, Gorky's general line deviated more and more from Lenin's directives. His doubts and scruples often won him the severe admonishments of the party, particularly in the case of something like his *Thoughts Out of Season* or *Two Souls.* Moreover, Bogdanov and old friends from Capri played a leading role on the editorial board of *Chronicles*, to the point of censoring Lenin himself. When Lenin, after thwarting the watchful eye of the authorities, managed to get an article to the magazine, he was asked to make changes in it! Outraged, he wrote a letter: "My manuscript on imperialism was able to reach Petersburg and there they inform me that the editor-in-chief (Gorky! the moron!) is displeased with my charges against . . . against whom, of all people? . . . Kautsky! It seems that he wants to write me about this. It is unfortunate and ridiculous."

The revolution broke out. But the thunderclap of October found Gorky wary. He dreaded the horrors of civil war, dictatorship, and terror; but he feared most of all the popular tidal wave that he saw approaching. Would the Soviets be able to bring it under control? The experience of blind mass brutality was too vivid in his memory and his worship of the values of civilization too great for him not to be disturbed. The honor of regenerating the world had fallen to the Russians and he was afraid. He wrote:

> . . . the weakest combatants, the least experienced, sons of a people who are economically and culturally backward, exhausted by a past more cruel than that of others, find themselves in the van of the nations in the final struggle for the triumph of justice. Just yesterday the world considered them half savages and today, almost dying from hunger, they march to victory or death, eagerly, forcefully, like proven warriors.

But would they hold out? Would they be able to win?

Gorky saw salvation only in an alliance of the working elite with the intellectual forces of the country, that is, with the

Cover of the first *Anthology of Proletarian Writers;* with a preface by Maxim Gorky, "Priboi" Editions, St. Petersburg, 1914.

liberal intelligentsia of the teachers and technicians. To him the revolution was possible only by reason of the cultural elevation of the people. He preached, therefore, the democratization of learning and the safeguarding of civilized values, "an immediate cultural construction, planned, diversified, resolute." In the middle of all the chaos he founded the "Free Association for the Development and Propagation of Positive Sciences," several "Leagues of Social Instruction," "Culture and Freedom," and particularly, the "Commission for the Protection of Museums, Art Works and Historical Monuments." Trotsky said: "Gorky welcomed the revolution with the misgivings of a museum director. Soldiers in stampede and laborers out of work terrified him."

In his daily, *New Life,* Gorky continued to engage in polemics with *Pravda,* to score "lynchings," and "the venom of power" which, he said, blinded Lenin and his cohorts and made them offer up the precious brain of the country as a sacrifice to the masses. In his Christmas supplement for 1917 he wrote: "Humanity's greatest creations are the two symbols which express its highest aspirations: Christ, the immortal idea of charity and mercy, and Prometheus, enemy of the gods, the first to revolt against destiny."

Lenin, for his part, had no time to go ahead with the education of the masses immediately. Yet Gorky went still further. He dreamed of a unified party of Bolsheviks and Mensheviks and declared that "it would be a fatal mistake to proclaim the Soviets straight off as the sole organ of revolutionary power." In March, 1918, the Soviet government banned his newspaper. Driven back to the social realm, Gorky took charge of the "Commission for the Improvement of Conditions of Scientists." He went to the aid of professors, writers, and technicians menaced in their physical and moral existence, committed to hunger and cold, and at the mercy of the political police. He forgot all old grudges and applied himself passionately to rescuing those who, in his eyes, personified civilization. Here is how the poet Hodasevitch described Gorky's day, in Petersburg, 1920:

> From morning to night his apartment did not empty. . . . He was beset by people come on all sorts of business: from the "House of Art," "House of Men of Letters," "House of Learning," and from "Universal Literature"; writers and

> scholars from Petersburg and elsewhere; workers and sailors ... artists, painters, speculators, former courtiers, ladies of quality. They begged him to intervene in indictments; thanks to him they obtained rations, lodgings, clothing, medicines, fats, railway tickets, travel orders, tobacco, paper, ink, false teeth for the old, milk for the newborn; in brief, everything that it was impossible to obtain without pull. Gorky listened to everyone and wrote innumerable letters of recommendation. Only once did I see him refuse a request: the clown Delvari wanted him at all cost to become the godfather of his baby....

At the same time, Gorky went on with his work as lecturer and technical adviser to new writers. Late in 1918 he had taken part in the creation of the first workers' and peasants' university, and his courses on the history of civilization were given just about everywhere, but mostly in the mobile proletarian university for workers and for sailors of the Red Navy.

A decided enemy of the regime of military communism, he conducted himself in opposition to the Soviet government. That gained him the mistrust and even the hostility of Lenin's followers, notably of Kamenev and Zinoviev. During the disastrous famine of 1919-20, Gorky for a time emerged from disfavor. The Soviet government, in the hope of obtaining the aid of western countries, sought to win allies among the intellectuals. Gorky, the friend and protector of the intellectuals, was well suited to serve as sponsor. Through his active efforts the "Pan-Russian Committee for Help to the Starving" was formed. There was a short period of liberalism, but very soon the Cheka put an end to it by shipping most of the members of the Committee off to jail. Gorky, in despair, accused Kamenev of having used him as a *provocateur*.

An outspoken and implacable friend of justice, untouchable because of his prestige and Lenin's friendship, Gorky had become altogether too much of a hindrance. And as his health was once again poor, Lenin stressed the necessity of his departure abroad where he could be cared for under conditions impossible in starving Russia. It took Lenin a long time and much persuasion to win Gorky's consent to leave, but finally in 1921 he gave in. The new exile was to last seven years.

Those seven years Gorky spent in a half-opposition to the Soviet regime, never breaking with it, never attacking it before

Europe, always hoping to see it become more humane. He even dreamed of being able to serve the regime, attempting in vain to act as the link between the Soviets and the Russian emigré writers.

In January, 1924, Lenin died, and Gorky, extremely suspicious of his successors, decided not to re-enter Russia. He wanted to return to Capri, but the Fascist government hesitated to let him come back to Italy. At last, in the spring, he was granted permission to take up residence not on Capri, where, Mussolini's authorities declared, "his presence might revive certain political feelings," but . . . in Sorrento, apparently

Sorrento, 1926-27.

politically reliable! Gorky stayed there for four years, leading the same simple, hard-working existence he had always known. But the old drama started over again: the writer was torn by homesickness. His Capri exile had been hard for the forty-year-old man, but the Sorrento exile, with the approach of his sixtieth year, was unbearable. Besides, this exile was senseless; the revolution had come. An expressive and touchingly sad image has come down to us from this period.

Interminable negotiations went on between Gorky – or rather his entourage – and the Soviets, and when at last he decided to return to the U.S.S.R., the White emigrés accused him of "selling himself to the devil." In a short letter to *Europe* (August 15, 1928), Gorky clarified his position:

> I have considered myself a "Bolshevik" since 1903, but I have never belonged to any party. . . . I made war on the Bolsheviks and I disputed with them in 1918; it seemed to me that they would be incapable of controlling the peasants, turned wild by the war and that, in struggling against them, they would sacrifice the workers' party. Then I became convinced of my mistake, and today I am persuaded that the Russian people, in spite of the war that the governments of Europe are waging against them and the economic difficulties resulting from it, have just crossed the threshold of their renaissance."

Later on, Gorky was to explain himself many times on this point, especially in his reminiscences of Lenin (the essential parts of which will be found at the end of this volume); but his most moving admission was contained in a letter to Professor Gruzdev, dated April 19, 1933:

> It is an established fact that the "theoretician" Lenin knew Russian reality infinitely better than I. . . . It seems to me that the "divergence" between us lies not just in the breadth of the conception and the unshakable integrity of the theory, but in something that could be called the lofty point of view. This is possible only with a rare gift: being able to consider the present from the vantage point of the future.

1928

THE PROLETARIAN WRITER

On October 22, 1927, the Communist Academy, supreme organ of Soviet thought, meeting in solemn session on the occasion of the thirty-fifth anniversary of Maxim Gorky's literary activity (he was still in Sorrento), opened a debate on the writer's proletarian quality. The discussion bore on two main points: the influence exerted by Gorky on Soviet literature and the social quality of his work. As the speakers followed one another, the problem emerged as follows: although Gorky deserved to be called a proletarian writer, it was extremely difficult, if not impossible, to prove objectively that he was one.

Actually, both in his person and in his art, he strayed from official doctrine, which required that a proletarian writer belong to the working class by his origins, his subjects, his protagonists, his style, and his philosophy.

Gorky fulfilled none of these conditions.

In his origins he was descended from peasant-artisans of the petty bourgeoisie; as for himself, during the course of his tumultuous youth, he had been an errand boy, ragpicker, cook's boy, bird-catcher, store clerk, apprentice designer, icon painter, stevedore, baker, bricklayer, watchman, railroad worker, lawyer's clerk, journalist, and man of letters, but at no time had he been an industrial worker.

His subject matter did not include pictures of factory life. Although he had mingled with scores of workmen, he was ignorant of factory life. Even in *The Mother* the action unfolded far from the work bench. Its protagonists and those of *Enemies,* not to mention others, were never real workers; they formed rather a sort of pre-proletariat, made up of uprooted peasants not yet recruited into factory work. Gorky contributed to the definition of this category of men by the term "okurovism" – from his novel *Okurov Town*, where the characters belonged to this "transitional period." The only class, properly speaking, that Gorky undertook to portray was the bourgeois intelligentsia, and that was certainly not proletarian either.

As for the writer's style, even though he followed the great national tradition of realism to the point of making almost the whole of his work a fictionalized reporting dominated by the autobiographical element, this realism was appreciably enhanced by romanticism.

And finally, the only philosophy that Gorky ever tried to formulate in any coherent manner was that of the "building of God," a notoriously "deviationist" theme. Gorky's hero *par excellence* was a man without ties, with the soul of a vagabond in search of that truth called God or justice. As violent as the social revolt of this hero may have been, it involved a fundamental popular religiosity or at least morality, right down through Vlassov, the model proletarian in *The Mother*, who declared to his judges – that is, to his class enemies – that he pitied them deeply, for in condemning him they were committing a crime against morality!

As a result of the reports, the Communist Academy found that in spite of the flagrant contradictions between the doctrine and his writing, the workers nonetheless felt Gorky to be *their* writer.

Several months after this debate, Gorky re-entered the U.S.S.R. He was given a hero's welcome, and crowned, with no possible objection, proletarian writer and creator of Soviet literature. The government awarded him the Order of Lenin, made him a member of the Central Executive Committee of the U.S.S.R., and a member of the Lenin Academy; his native town of Nizhni Novgorod was renamed Gorky. The trend was followed by many clubs, schools, factories, and theaters adopting the name of Gorky, including the Moscow Art Theater

Gorky in the wings of the Moscow Art Theater,
between Stanislavsky (at right) and the actor, Kachalov.

which had performed his first plays. And last, the supreme glorification, the Moscow Institute of Literature was to receive his name. After that, any debate like the one which had taken place at the Communist Academy was out of the question. Under Stalin's instigation, undoubtedly, Gorky's glory entered what might be called an autocratic phase.

Now in his sixties, however, in the eight years of work remaining to him he created nothing which modified the former characteristics of his work. Novelist, he remained bound to the same subjects, continuing to depict intellectuals in *Klim Samgin* (1924-36). Playwright, in *Iegor Bulychov* (1931), *Dostigaiev and Others* (1933), or the new versions of earlier plays *(Vassa Zheleznova, The Old Man*, etc.), he continued to dramatize the same fallen, middle-class heroes, struggling with the same dramatic family situations. Journalist, he still dealt with the old themes, but his polemic against Western Europe, America, the middle class, and capitalism, as vicious as it was, did not exceed the brutality of his pamphlets of 1906.

And last of all, in his pedagogic and social activity, Gorky remained attached to the same goals of education. But from then on, his powers in this domain were limitless.

If Gorky himself did nothing really new, there was a new interpretation given his work which made it appear in greater conformity to official doctrine. He was pronounced "classic" and an entire Gorky-literature was created, made up of monographs and studies intended on the one hand to minimize the writer's various "deviations," and on the other hand to establish "concordances" between his works and Marxist writings. Thus, not only could it no longer be declared in Russia – up until the new order – that *Klim Samgin* was a manifest failure, as had been said more than once prior to 1928, but this novel was presented as a function of the "ideologic belief of Gorky," testifying to the fact that the writer had usefully assimilated the advice of Lenin and Stalin.

Lenin was unhampered by literary theories, when, starting with the beginning of the century, he had called for "a party literature." He wanted incendiary stuff able to "raise the consciousness of the workers," that would awaken, move, prod to action. Gorky reasoned no differently. Questioned by a group of workers, he answered them: "Personally I am not interested in the disputes of the critics as to whether I am a 'proletarian or non-proletarian writer.' In the mass of congratulations I am getting from workmen in every corner of the Union they call me with one voice 'our own,' 'proletarian,' and 'comrade.' The voice of the workmen is, of course, more imposing to me than the critics' voices."

And he gave his definition, which had nothing to do with the "objective criteria" of the doctrine. For Gorky, the writer was proletarian when he hated "everything that oppresses man from the outside and from within, everything that prevents the free development and growth of man's faculties"; when he respected man "as the source of creative energy, the creator of all things, of all wonders of the earth"; when he lyricized "collective labor, which aims to create news forms of life"; when he saw woman "as not only the source of physiological enjoyment, but as a faithful comrade and helpmate in the difficult business of life"; and children as "persons before whom we are all responsible for everything we do." In short, the writer was "proletarian" if he "activated" his reader, if he dragged him into the fight and made him understand the greatness of militant commitment.

In the face of this definition, the problems of "origins," "subjects," "philosophy," and the sterile controversy of "socialist realism" lost all importance.

In effect, socialist realism, whatever its definitions and redefinitions, was scarcely any of Gorky's doing. Paradoxically, if his realism, which drew upon the great national tradition, did have an impact, it was due to the romanticism with which it was strongly tinged.

"The positive hero!" Gorky spoke passionately of him to the young people, but he knew only how to paint fantastic vagabonds or wayward intellectuals. (None of his "good" proletarians have been successful.) By instinct, Gorky followed the inexorable literary law which, in memory of the great poet of the *Inferno* who failed to reach Heaven, one might call "Dante's Law." Gorky's understanding of men was infinite and he loved them as they were with their defects and their weaknesses. "If there is anything on earth sacred and great it is the incessant growth of man, precious even when it is hateful!" Having proposed to write "a book about Russians as they had been," he changed his mind: "I am not quite certain of my own feelings: do I wish people to become different?" What had to change were the atrocious conditions of their lives. That is why, wherever he was or whatever he did, Gorky's "negative" hero, complex, tormented, contradictory, was an instrument of demolition of the old world, a revolutionary explosive. "Well, where then is the call to revolt in *The Lower Depths*?" asked a group of Red Guardsmen. "In Satin's appreciation of men!" replied Gorky. For against a flophouse background of complete degradation, Satin exclaimed, "MAN – that has a proud ring!"

This motif, this motto, if you wish, recurred throughout Gorky's work; he cast it in simple symbols on which the crowd fed. In it lay the unprecedented success of his prose poems: Man, creator, king of nature; the impassioned heart torn from the chest, serving as a torch along the roads of the future; the falcon going into battle against raging forces (symbolized by the eel), ready to spill his warm and noble blood; and at last, the petrel, the herald of the storm, and the waves singing "the madness of the brave."

Gorky's man, weak and faulty, but burning with a spiritual thirst and experiencing in his misery gleams of supreme joy, that man is the eternal hero of Russian literature. We undoubtedly owe to this Russian hero all the excitement produced by the invasion of this literature into the West at the end of the nineteenth century. Smack in the middle of the progressive, positivist euphoria of a particularly rational period, Russia thrust once more the theme of eternal human restlessness. In returning to it, Gorky, by his very limitations, simplified its fundamental ideas and put them before a new public, inexperienced in art, but thirsting for contact with humanity. "Russian art," said Gorky, "is above all else an art of the soul." No doubt that was the reason why, out of many works in Russia which conformed to doctrine, Gorky's continued to break all records for publishing and theatrical performances. It allowed the worker to escape from the mechanization of a "positive" literature in progressing towards humanism – in the sense bestowed on the word by the great Swiss Hellenist, André Bonnard, who spoke of "Soviet humanism"; a "frenzy for knowledge," a "passion for understanding," an approach to literature as "the science of man, the education of man."

Italy, 1931.

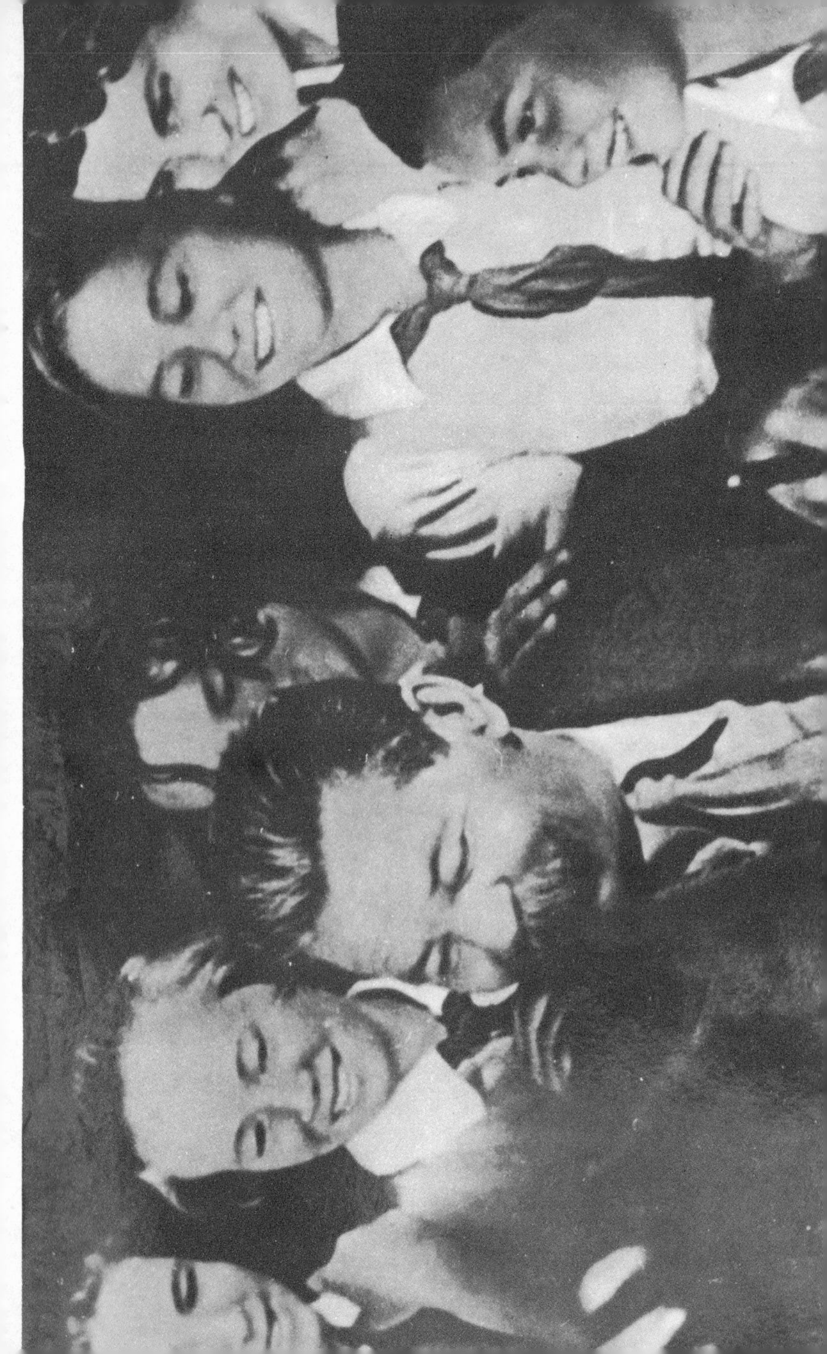

THE MAN AND THE MASTER

Seven years earlier Gorky had left a country smoking in ruins, only just beginning to dress the wounds caused by famine and civil war. But in ten years a tremendous work of reconstruction had been accomplished. He roamed throughout the Union, looking and questioning. As a man who had worked in the mines and in the oil fields, he was astounded by the new mining villages, the child-care nurseries, the schools, and the living conditions of workers no longer ignorant of comfort and hygiene. This man who had known wracking physical effort, now saw the machine in the social role of a working partner. The grandson of a Volga boatman, how could he have failed to be impressed by the Dnieprostroy Dam? A former prison-baker, how could he not have wept when he saw the mechanized bakery in Leningrad – everything white, clean, and ventilated? To these happy, healthy bakers he said:

"In my time, we worked eighteen to twenty hours a day."

"And we work only seven," they answered.

Perhaps at that moment there echoed in Gorky's memory one of the most beautiful pages he had written, the opening of *Twenty-Six and One*.

> There were twenty-six of us – twenty-six living machines, locked up in a damp cellar, where we patted dough from morning till night. . . . The windows of our cellar looked out into a ditch . . . the light of the sun could not peep in through the panes. . . . It was stifling and narrow in our box of stone under the low, heavy ceiling, covered with smoke-black and spider-webs. It was close and disgusting within the thick walls, which were spattered with stains of mud and mustiness. . . .

And it was certainly with all his heart that he wrote in the visitor's book: "This factory is the most wonderful thing I have seen in Leningrad. There is nothing which bears more eloquent witness to the revolution accomplished in everyday living."

You have to read Gorky's work to understand just how inevitable the revolution was, and why, starting at so backward a level, it had to assume such cruel forms.

He never stopped comparing. What was *now* took on meaning only in light of what had been *before*.

At a solemn session of the Baku Soviet, he said:

> Perhaps the young people don't like to hear me hark back so often to the past? I do it deliberately. It seems to me that youth is not familiar enough with this past, that they don't visualize clearly enough the tortured and heroic lives of their fathers, nor the conditions under which they labored, until those days when their organized will overturned and smashed the old regime. I know that my memory is overloaded with "old relics," but I can forget nothing, and I cannot see that it should be forgotten. . . .

If he referred to himself it was not because his personal past haunted him:

> I talk too much about myself? It's quite true. But what else can I do? I have witnessed the struggle between the old and the new. I am testifying in the tribunal of history before the laboring youth whose appalling ignorance of the evil past hinders them from fully appreciating the present with which they are none too familiar.

Maxim Gorky didn't matter, what was important was "the case of Maxim Gorky," which was not an exception, because it had been the case of millions of small boys given severe beatings by their grandfathers. And yet these grandfathers were not mean. It was just that they did not understand that their cruelty was the unleashing of the terrible and impotent anger of people who did not yet know where or whom to strike.

> If I were a critic and had to write on Maxim Gorky, I should say that the force which made him what he is, such as he is here before you, the writer that you love and appreciate so exaggeratedly, well, I should say that this force derives from his having been the first among Russian writers and perhaps the first in general to have understood, directly and unaided, the tremendous value of work; work, creator of all that is beautiful, great, and precious in this world.

For Gorky, the essence of the revolution, the essence of Soviet power lay in the advancement of men. The emigrés accused him of having sold himself for glory or for a mirage? Certainly not!

> The authors of anonymous letters [he replied] want to know why I do not say now what I said in 1917. My reply is that in 1917 I was mistaken, sincerely fearing that the dictatorship of the proletariat would lead to the dispersion and destruction of the politically trained Bolshevik workers, the only real revolutionary force, and that their destruction would result in the eclipse for a long time to come of the very idea of a social revolution. . . . I do not flatter the workers' and peasants' regime; I sincerely admire its work and its ability to inspire people to work and creative activity.

He dedicated himself thereafter to the task of "inspiring," of educating the young people on the social and literary plane. In this, he was only continuing a labor which had always excited him. More than all the other honors bestowed on him, Gorky deserved the title "master," in the purest and noblest sense of the word. It would be difficult to find a man of letters who has so sincerely, so ardently shared with young people his knowledge, his time, an his experience. The miracle of this man, said one of his "disciples," was "his tenderness, his words

ЧЕЛКАШЪ.

(1894—1895)

Потемнѣвшее отъ пыли голубое южное небо—мутно; жаркое солнце смотритъ въ зеленоватое море, точно сквозь тонкую сѣрую вуаль. Оно не отражается въ водѣ, разсѣкаемой ударами веселъ, пароходныхъ винтовъ, острыми килями турецкихъ фелюгъ и другихъ судовъ, бороздящихъ по всѣмъ направленіямъ тѣсную гавань. Закованныя въ гранитъ волны моря, подавленныя громадными тяжестями, скользящими по ихъ хребтамъ, бьются о борта судовъ, о берега, бьются и ропщутъ, вспѣненныя, загрязненныя разнымъ хламомъ.

Звонъ якорныхъ цѣпей, грохотъ сцѣпленій вагоновъ, подвозящихъ грузъ, металлическій вопль желѣзныхъ листовъ, откуда-то падающихъ на камень мостовой, глухой стукъ дерева, дребезжаніе извозчичьихъ телѣгъ, свистки пароходовъ, то пронзительно рѣзкіе, то глухо ревущіе, крики грузчиковъ, матросовъ и таможенныхъ солдатъ,—всѣ эти звуки сливаются въ оглушительную музыку трудового дня и, мятежно колыхаясь, стоятъ въ небѣ надъ гаванью, къ нимъ вздымаются съ земли все новыя и новыя волны—то глухія, рокочущія, онѣ сурово сотрясаютъ все кругомъ, то рѣзкія, гремящія,—рвутъ пыльный, знойный воздухъ.

which scarcely sounded like the responses of a famous writer to a beginner, and which Gorky found for countless persons and continued to find in his heart as long as it beat."

Gorky's heart! Tolstoy understood it when he said to the young writer: "You are funny – don't be offended – very funny. And it's very strange that you should still be good-natured when you might well be spiteful. . . . Your mind I don't understand – it's a very tangled mind – but your heart is sensible. . . ."

Gorky never ceased to be roused by the problems of beginners. In 1911 he published a curious article, "Self-Taught Writers," in which he summarized the results of his having combed through more than 400 manuscripts sent to him on Capri by writers of the people. Gorky had very carefully read, annotated, and classified them. Among the authors, the workers led, with 114 manuscripts; then came the peasants, 67; the remainder was a mixed group, nine shoemakers, six houseporters, five soldiers, four tailors, four former convicts, five seamstresses, three maids, two prostitutes, one laundress, one cemetery watchman, one police agent, and so on. Out of 429 manuscripts, only 67 stories and 6 plays were devoted to the revolution; of these, the majority were written not in prose but in verse.

In 1914, Gorky took a great step forward with the publication of the first *Anthology of Proletarian Writers*. In his preface he called attention to the technical weaknesses of the authors, and not content with rousing the creative power of the workers, he called on them to learn the craft of writing, and not to be lured by the hope of creating a new proletarian literature without a knowledge of the craft itself. Study! This was the advice he lavished untiringly on the young people.

During his second exile in Sorrento, Gorky repeated his Capri experience. In 1927, in his "Reader's Notes," he reviewed two hundred books by young Soviet authors whom he sought to understand and guide. On his return to Russia, he threw himself into the increasing literary activity; he read manuscripts, wrote prefaces, corrected, explained, and discussed line by line. And, unable to write to each individual, he wrote collective letters to the various groups: beginners, readers, worker and peasant correspondents, publishing houses, adult schools, teachers (concerning juvenile literature which interested him immensely), printers, railway workers, Red Guards, the literary and dramatic groups of workers' clubs, etc. Or

Page from the story *Chelkash* prepared by Gorky for its first post-revolutionary edition; the corrections are in the new orthography.

else he published articles, delivered lectures and wrote pamphlets, the most famous of which was *How I Became a Writer* (1928), through which he wanted to help beginners profit from his own experience, thus saving them waste of energy and needless gropings.

A huge daily undertaking, unceasing, humble, serving modest ends, none of which can be considered insignificant: this was Gorky's work during his last years. We are in the presence of one of the finest efforts known to the history of letters, an effort which was crowned by the founding of *Literary Apprenticeship*, a magazine which proposed "to teach beginning writers the literary alphabet, the craft, and the power of the word," and the establishment of an institute of literature which was appropriately named the Gorky Institute.

Through this tremendous work Gorky attained greatness. One can understand Chekhov's saying: "I think that a time will come when Gorky's works will be forgotten, but it is doubtful that even in a thousand years Gorky, the man, will be forgotten."

In the midst of all his glory, the writer remained infinitely modest. Though he referred to himself constantly, it was not at all with the idea of analyzing himself. On the contrary, this author of so vast a body of work in which the biographical element was so important, was exceptional in taking no interest in his "I." If he wrote from time to time that "his soul hurt him," or that he was sad and disgusted, it was always in terms of specific externals, stemming from a detestable social order which he was out to destroy. He spoke not in order to show his "I" was distinguished from others, but in order to give reassurance, because he was like everybody else. Never at any time in his life did this man of unparalleled fame give way to vanity.

It is, therefore, all the more important to give short shrift to a legend for which Gorky was not responsible and which throws a shadow of undeserved ridicule over his memory.

On October 11, 1931, Stalin and Voroshilov paid a visit to the writer. On this occasion, he read to them one of the "atrocities" of his youth, the poem, "The Young Girl and Death" (1892). Across the page of the book Stalin wrote a sort of facetious testimonial which he signed and dated: "This

VII.

Смерть молчит, а девушкины речи
Зависти огнем ей кости плавят,
В жар и холод властно ее мечут,
Что же сердце Смерти миру явит?
Смерть — не мать, но — женщина, и в ней
Сердце тоже разума сильней;
В темном сердце Смерти есть ростки
Жалости и гнева и тоски.
Тем, кого она полюбит крепче,
Кто ужален в душу злой тоскою,
Как она любовно ночью шепчет
О великой радости покоя!
— «Что ж, — сказала Смерть, — пусть будет чудо!
Разрешаю я тебе — живи!
Только я с тобою рядом буду,
Вечно буду около Любви!»

С той поры Любовь и Смерть, как сестры,
Ходят неразлучно до сего дня,
За Любовью Смерть с косою острой
Тащится повсюду, точно сводня.
Ходит, околдована сестрою,
И везде — на свадьбе и на тризне
Неустанно, неуклонно строит
Радости Любви и счастье Жизни.

56

Эта штука сильнее чем "Фауст" Гете (любовь побеждает смерть)
11/X-31 г.
И. Сталин

If Gorky, who was not bald, appears to be here, it is because he is wearing a skull-cap.

piece is greater than Goethe's *Faust*. Love conquers death."

We say facetious, first, because of its style, and second, because it is unthinkable that Gorky, as we know him, who ranked among the greatest geniuses of mankind, could have taken Stalin's note seriously. A photograph exists which seems to tie in with the October 11 visit. It shows Stalin, Voroshilov, and Gorky, the latter examining an open book, and all three bursting with laughter. It's caption could be, "That's a good one!"

At any rate, Gorky put away the book bearing Stalin's inscription and that was the end of it. Seventeen years later someone put his hand on Stalin's "testimonial" and gave it the widest publicity. The reproduction of the fateful page appeared in the new *Great Soviet Encyclopedia*, in the *Complete Works of Gorky*, and in numerous magazines and articles. An official painter even made a painting of it in which Gorky, in a pathetic pose, was reading his work to Stalin and Voroshilov (the painter went so far as to add Molotov). This discovery obviously could not have been spread abroad without the consent of Stalin, whose praise – judging from what we know of his taste – might have been perfectly sincere. Gorky was no longer there to defend himself. And so the Soviet critics pretended to take it seriously, to the great joy of the emigrés who were free to deplore barbarism. But the final blow was dealt by *Europe* (lead item in No. 57, September, 1950) which, not content with piously reproducing Stalin's "literary judgment," accompanied it with the text of the poem itself. The translation repaired the poor construction of the poem, but was unable to conceal its poverty.

Even in Soviet literature, which is generally rather discreet concerning the intimate affairs of authors, few writers have defended "the wall of privacy" as fiercely as Gorky. His many autobiographical stories made no mention of his private life, with the exception of his first love, Madame Kaminskaia, who followed him to Nizhni Novgorod in 1892. Even then it was as a series of "tragic-comic emotions" that he described the tiffs between himself and this "lady of my heart" as he called her, gay, cynical, and cultivated. She courageously shared the poverty of a young journalist earning two kopeks a line; she made hats, and did portraits of priests and their wives; she talked to Gorky about her visit to Paris, of poets whom he did

Gorky with Madame Catherine Peshkov and their children,
Maxim and Katioucha: Nizhni Novgorod, 1903.

not understand, and of a distant sparkling world. Gorky wrote without rancor of how she fell asleep while he was reading one of his stories to her. These two people had very little in common and they separated without any dramatic complications.

With his son Maxim, 1899.

With his son in Paris, 1912.

He married in Nizhni Novgorod. Madame Catherine Peshkov was a typical Russian intellectual and an ardent revolutionary. They didn't stay together for more than a few years. Madame Peshkov bore him two children: their daughter Katioucha died young, and little Maxim became a carefree good-for-nothing, whose father always remained devoted to him.

During the time of his theatrical successes Gorky had come to know Madame Maria Andreyeva, who was to accompany him to America and Capri. At the time of the revolution she was succeeded by the troublesome Baroness Moura Budberg, who had a talent for making herself disliked by the writer's friends. Born into the *beau monde* of Petersburg, she spoke several languages extremely well and Russian with an English accent. She was the companion of his second exile. Actually, the only woman Gorky spoke of with tenderness and without reservation was the "Queen Margot" of his adolescence, of whom he had made an unattainable ideal.

Despite his many raw descriptions of sexual excesses, there is a temptation to accuse Gorky of prudishness. It was – and the Frenchman Melchior de Vogué was keen enough to notice it more than the Russians – that he was conspicuously lacking in sensuality. His coarsely erotic scenes were always depicted with a moralizing intent which cooled the reader. Gorky was chaste to the point of substituting the word "joys" for "pleasure." Often in his stories we see the narrator acting naively, out of pure nobility of soul, which does not necessarily save him from appearing ridiculous. When, in *The Confession,* he consented to have a child by a lovely young novice who thereby hoped to be expelled from the convent where she had been forcibly imprisoned, he did so reluctantly and only through a feeling of humanity. It was always a question with him of the "sacrament of marriage."

What were Gorky's last years like? Did he adhere completely to the Soviet regime or did he argue, protest, contradict? Did he really fill with complaints several fat notebooks which disappeared mysteriously after his death? We know nothing of all this. The bewildering official communiqué of March 3, 1938, lent credibility to the rumors. Two years after the author's death, which occurred on June 18, 1936 following a bout of pneumonia, the communiqué declared that he had been "medically assassinated" by his attending physicians, on the order of Yagoda, chief of the Cheka. It further specified that Gorky's son, the happy-go-lucky and harmless Maxim, whose death – also following a seizure of pneumonia – had preceded his father's by one year, was himself a victim of the same conspiracy.

As monstrous as it was incredible, just how much was this accusation worth? Its resemblance to the case of the doctors accused of similar crimes on January 13, 1953, this time on Beria's instigation, and then reinstated upon Stalin's death, makes the affair suspicious. In the absence of reliable evidence, let us refrain from all suppositions. Whatever the Soviet government's reasons for surrounding the controversial writer with surveillance, something even Lenin had not contrived to do, it is possible that a 68-year-old man, in whom pneumonia was sapping a body shaken by fifty years of tuberculosis, could have died a natural death. One can only deplore the suspicion thrown on the last hours of one of the purest, most unselfish men that the world of letters has ever known.

While placing himself at the opposite literary pole, Alexander Blok felt it deeply when he said:

> If there is something great, boundless, vast, painfully gripping and promising which we have been wont to associate with the name of Russia, then it is Gorky whom we must regard as having best expressed all that.

Gorky was twenty-five years old when, in an autobiographical note, he made his first attempt to define a meaning for his life:

STATEMENT OF THE THOUGHTS AND ACTS WHOSE MUTUAL ACTION HAS DETERMINED THE WITHERING OF SOME OF THE FINEST PARTS OF MY SOUL.

In the year 1868, on the 14th day of the month of March, at 2 o'clock in the morning, as a result of her predilection for bad jokes, as well as a finishing touch to the mass of absurdities that she has committed at various times, nature had me born with one objective stroke of the brush.

Despite the importance of this event, I have not the slightest personal memory of it, but grandmother has told me that at the minute human spirit was conferred upon me, I uttered a cry.

I choose to believe that it was a cry of indignation and protest. (1893)

MY CHILDHOOD

In a narrow, darkened room, my father, dressed in a white and unusually long garment, lay on the floor under the window. The toes of his bare feet were curiously extended, and the fingers of the still hands, which rested peacefully upon his breast, were curved; his merry eyes were tightly closed by the black disks of two copper coins; the light had gone out of his still face, and I was frightened by the ugly way he showed his teeth.

With those caressing hands, and those laughing eyes, went Alexei's happy childhood. From Astrakhan, he and his mother went to Nizhni Novgorod, to live with the family of his maternal grandfather.

Then began the astonishingly rapid flow of an intense, varied, inexpressibly strange life. It reminded me of a crude story, well told by a good-natured but irritatingly truthful genius.

My grandfather's house simply seethed with mutual hostility; all the grown people were infected and even the children were inoculated with it. I had learned, from overhearing grandmother's conversation, that my mother came back home upon the very day when her brothers demanded the distribution of the property left by their father. Her un-

His grandfather's house where Gorky lived as a child.

expected return made their desire for this all the keener and stronger, because they were afraid that my mother would claim the dowry intended for her, but withheld by my grandfather because she had married secretly and against his wish.

Grandfather was a short, wizened man, dressed in black, with a red-gold beard, a bird-like nose, and green eyes. . . . I did not like either the grown-up people or the children; I felt myself to be a stranger in their midst. . . . Most of all I disliked my uncle; I felt at once that he was my enemy, and I was conscious of a certain feeling of cautious curiosity towards him. . . . I was very well aware that grandfather's shrewd, sharp green eyes followed me everywhere. . . .

His first mischief led to his punishment in a wild scene; the child was torn from the hands of his hysterical mother and grandmother.

Grandfather flogged me till I lost consciousness, and I was unwell for some days, tossing about, face downwards, on a wide, stuffy bed, in a little room with one window and a lamp which was always kept burning before the group of icons in the corner.

Those dark days had been the greatest in my life. In the course of them I had developed wonderfully, and I was conscious of a peculiar difference in myself. I began to experience a new solicitude for others, and I became so keenly alive to their sufferings and my own that it was almost as if my heart had been lacerated, and thus rendered sensitive.

But the old man told Alexei about his own youth, as a Volga boatman, dragging the barges on foot. . . .

". . . in the water, and I ran barefoot on the bank, which was strewn with sharp stones. . . . Thus I went from early in the morning to sunset, with the sun beating fiercely on the back of my neck, and my head throbbing as if it were full of molten iron . . . my poor little bones ached, but I had to keep on, and I could not see the way; and then my eyes brimmed over, and I sobbed my heart out as the tears rolled down. Ah! Oleysha! it won't bear talking about.

"I went on and on till the towing-rope slipped from me and I fell down on my face, and I was not sorry for it either! I rose up all the stronger. If I had not rested a minute I

Volga boatmen (drawing by Repin).

should have died. That is the way we used to live then in the sight of God and of our Blessed Lord Jesus Christ....

"Well, sometimes, Oleysha, on a summer's evening when we arrived at Jigulak, or some such place at the foot of the green hills, we used to sit lazily cooking our supper while the boatmen of the hill-country used to sing sentimental songs, and as soon as they began the whole crew would strike up, sending a thrill through one, and making the Volga seem as if it were running very fast like a horse, and rising up as high as the clouds; and all kinds of trouble seemed as nothing more than dust blown about by the wind."

He stayed with me and told me stories until it was almost dark, and when, after an affectionate farewell, he left me, I had learned that he was neither malevolent nor formidable. It brought the tears into my eyes to remember that it was he who had so cruelly beaten me, but I could not forget it.

One after another, violent scenes took place, culminating in the ugly killing of an adopted child, by the uncles in the family. And yet, there were days when Uncle Jacob, treacherous, greedy, sneaky, a man who had tortured his wife to death, would tear at his own face, beat his temples and his chest, pull out his hair, and claw at his lips in penitence. And then, there was his music:

Uncle Jacob tuned his guitar amorously.... His music demanded an intense silence. It rushed like a rapid torrent from somewhere far away, stirring one's heart and penetrating it with an incomprehensible sensation of sadness and uneasiness. Under the influence of that music we all became melancholy, and the oldest present felt themselves to be no more than children. We sat perfectly still – lost in a dreamy silence.

All this was extremely interesting, and held me spellbound, and filled my heart with a tender, not unpleasant sadness. For sadness and gladness live within us side by side, almost inseparable; the one succeeding the other with an elusive, unappreciable swiftness.

And above all there was grandmother...

...the person who introduced me into this fascinating, though difficult life, life in the world. When I remember her all the badness and all the hurts become blurred, every-

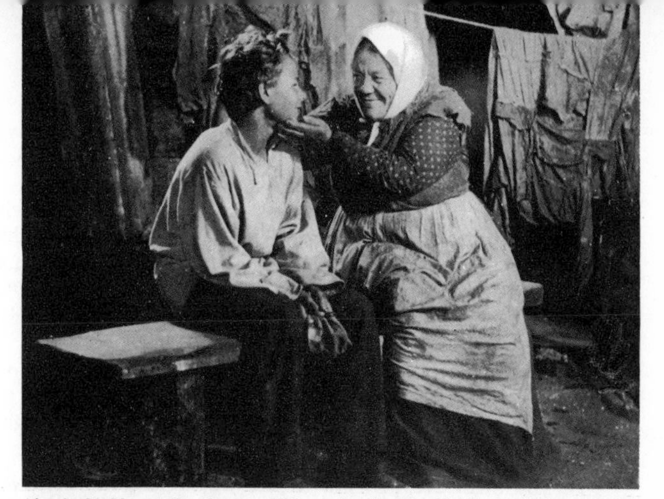

Alexei with his grandmother (a still from the film *The Childhood of Maxim Gorky*).

thing alters and becomes more attractive, more interesting, men seem better. . . .

She always talked using such peculiarly harmonious words that they took root in my memory like fragrant, bright, everlasting flowers. When she smiled the pupils of her dark, luscious eyes dilated and beamed with an inexpressible charm, and her strong white teeth gleamed cheerfully. Apart from her multitudinous wrinkles and her swarthy complexion, she had a youthful and brilliant appearance. What spoiled her was her bulbous nose, with its red nostrils distended by her habit of taking pinches of snuff from her black snuff-box mounted with silver. . . . Everything about her was dark, but within she was luminous with an inextinguishable, joyful, and ardent flame, which revealed itself in her eyes. Although she was bent – almost humpbacked, in fact – she moved lightly and softly, for all the world like a huge cat, and was just as gentle as that caressing animal.

Until she came into my life I seemed to have been asleep, and hidden away in obscurity; but when she appeared she woke me and led me to the light of day. Connecting all my impressions by a single thread, she wove them into a pattern of many colors, thus making herself my friend for life, the being nearest my heart, the dearest and best known of all; while her disinterested love for all creation enriched me, and built up the strength needed for a hard life.

And taking a pinch of snuff, she would begin to tell me some wonderful stories about kind-hearted brigands, holy people, and all sorts of wild animals and evil spirits.

She would tell me these stories softly, mysteriously, with her face close to mine, fixing me with her dilated eyes, thus actually infusing into me strength which grew within me. The longer she spoke, or rather sang, the more melodiously flowed her words. It was inexpressibly pleasant to listen to her.

His mother's personal life, her departures and mysterious reappearances, weighed heavily on the boy's mind. But the moods of the household were changeable, and when the fights and quarrels were over, they all sat down around the table.

As the meal dragged out to the weary length which was usual on Sundays and holidays, it seemed to me that these could not be the same people who, only half an hour ago, were shouting at each other, on the verge of fighting, and bursting out into tears and sobs. I could not believe . . . that they were in earnest now, and that they were not ready to weep all the time. But those tears and cries, and the scenes which they inflicted upon one another, happened so often, and died away so quickly, that I began to get used to them, and they gradually ceased to excite me or to cause me heartache.

Much later I realized that Russian people, because of the poverty and squalor of their lives, love to amuse themselves with sorrow – to play with it like children, and are seldom ashamed of being unhappy.

Amidst their endless weekdays, grief makes a holiday, and a fire is an amusement – a scratch is an ornament to an empty face.

Grandfather's affairs took a turn for the worse, and he became more miserly. They had to move into a basement flat.

When we went to this lodging, grandmother took an old bast shoe, put it under the stove, and, squatting on her heels, invoked the house-demon:

"House-demon, family-demon, here is your sledge; come to us in our new home, and bring us good luck."

But grandfather, in a rage, forbade this "heresy." Things went from bad to worse.

I was not often allowed out in the street, and on each occasion I returned home bearing signs of having been knocked about by other boys; for fighting was my favorite, indeed, my only enjoyment, and I threw myself into it with ardor. Mother whipped me with a strap, but the punishment only irritated me further, and the next time I fought with childish fury – and mother gave me a worse punishment. This went on until one day I warned her that if she did not leave off beating me I should bite her hand, and run away to the fields and get frozen to death. She pushed me away from her in amazement, and walked about the room, panting from exhaustion as she said:

"You are getting like a wild animal!"

His mother remarried. The stepfather was dismissed from his job for having pilfered from the workmen, and Alexei found himself living in another basement.

As soon as she was settled mother sent me to school – and from the very first I took a dislike to it.

I went there in mother's shoes, with a coat made out of a bodice belonging to grandmother, a yellow shirt, and trousers which had been lengthened. My attire immediately became an object of ridicule, and for the yellow shirt I received "the ace of diamonds." *

I soon became friendly with the boys, but the master and the priest did not like me.

Alexei got back at the master with "savage pranks."

Notwithstanding the fact that I learned tolerably well, I was soon told that I should be expelled from school for unbecoming conduct. I became depressed, for I saw a very unpleasant time coming, as mother was growing more irritable every day, and beat me more than ever.

But help was at hand. Bishop Khrisanph paid an unexpected visit to the school. He was a little man, like a wizard, and, if I remember rightly, was humpbacked.

He had the boy recite episodes from scripture history and popular poems; Alexei knew quite a few of them thanks to his grandmother.

---

* The insignia that prisoners wore on their backs.

Placing his hand, which smelt of cypress wood, on my head he asked:

"Why are you so naughty?"

"It is so dull learning."

"Dull? Now, my boy, that is not true. If you found it dull you would be a bad scholar, whereas your teachers testify that you are a very apt pupil. That means that you have another reason for being naughty."

After having left instructions with the priest . . .

. . . he led me by the hand to the porch, where he said quietly,

"So you will restrain yourself, won't you? . . . I understand why you are naughty, you know. . . ."

I was very excited; my heart was seething with strange feelings, and when the teacher, having dismissed the rest of the class, kept me in to tell me that now I ought to be quieter than water and humbler than grass, I listened to him attentively and willingly.

One evening Alexei witnessed a scene between his mother and stepfather.

I heard him strike her, and rushing into the room I saw that mother, who had fallen onto her knees, was resting her back and elbows against a chair, with her chest forward and her head thrown back, with a rattling in her throat, and terribly glittering eyes; while he, dressed in his best, with a new overcoat, was kicking her in the chest with his long foot. I seized a knife from the table – a knife with a bone handle set in silver, which they used to cut bread, the only thing belonging to my father which remained to mother – and I seized it and struck with all my force at my stepfather's side.

By good luck mother was in time to push Maximov away, and the knife going sideways tore a wide hole in his overcoat, and only grazed his skin. My stepfather, gasping, rushed from the room holding his side, and mother seized me and lifted me up; then with a groan threw me on the floor. My stepfather took me away from her when he returned from the yard.

Late that evening, when, in spite of everything, he had gone out, mother came to me behind the stove, gently took me in her arms, kissed me, and said, weeping:

"Forgive me; it was my fault! Oh, my dear, how could you! . . . And with a knife?"

I remember with perfect clearness how I said to her that I would kill my stepfather and myself too. And I think I should have done it; at any rate I should have made the attempt. Even now I can see that contemptible long leg, in braided trousers, flung out into the air and kicking a woman's breast.

As I remember these oppressive horrors of our wild Russian life, I often ask myself whether it is worth while to speak of them. And then, with restored confidence, I answer myself: "It is worth while because it is actual, vile fact, which has not died out, even in these days – a fact which must be traced to its origin, and pulled up by the root from the memories, the souls of the people, and from our narrow, sordid lives."

Once more Alexei found himself at his grandparents'.

I also began to earn a little money; on holidays, early in the morning, I took a bag and went about the yards and streets collecting bones, rags, paper, and nails. Rag-merchants would give me two greevin (twenty kopeks) for a pood (forty pounds) of rags and paper, or iron, and ten or eight kopeks for a pood of bones. I did this work on weekdays after school, too, and on Saturdays I sold the articles at thirty kopeks or half a ruble each, and sometimes more if I was lucky. Grandmother took the money away from me and put it quietly into the pocket of her skirt, and praised me, looking down:

"There! Thank you, my darling. This will do for our food. . . . You have done very well."

One day I saw her holding five kopeks of mine in her hands, looking at them, and quietly crying; and one muddy tear hung from the tip of her grainy nose, that looked like a pumice stone.

A more lucrative source of revenue than rag-picking was the theft of logs and planks from the warehouses along the river.

I managed to pick up some friendly accomplices – one ten-year-old son of a Mordvin beggar, Sanka Vyakhir, a kind, gentle boy always tranquilly happy; kinless Kostrom, lanky and lean, with tremendous black eyes, who in his thirteenth year was sent to a colony of young criminals for stealing a pair of doves; the little Tartar Khabi, a twelve-year-old "strong man," simple-minded and kind; blunt-nosed Yaz, the son of a graveyard watchman and gravedigger, a boy of eight, taciturn as a fish, and suffering from epilepsy; and the eldest of all was the son of a widowed dressmaker, Grishka Tchurka, a sensible, straightforward boy, who was terribly handy with his fists. We all lived in the same street.

My life at school had again become hard; the pupils nicknamed me "The Ragman" and "The Tramp," and one day, after a quarrel, they told the teacher that I smelt like a sewer, and that they could not sit beside me. I remember how deeply this accusation cut me, and how hard it was for me to go to school after it. The complaint had been made up out of malice. I washed very thoroughly every morning, and I never want to school in the clothes I wore when I was collecting rags.

However, in the end I passed the examination for the third class, and received as prizes bound copies of the Gospels and the *Fables of Krilov*, and another book, unbound, which bore the unintelligible title of *Fata-Morgana*; they also gave me some sort of laudatory certificate.

I took the books to a little shop, where I sold them for fifty-five kopeks, and gave the money to grandmother; as to the certificate, I spoiled it by scribbling over it, and then handed it to grandfather, who took it without turning it over, and so put it away, without noticing the mischief I had done.

School was over and he returned to the streets. But Alexei's mother, whose husband had disappeared, came back to live with her parents, and he took care of his baby brother, a weak, scrofulous baby who was soon to die. One Sunday morning in August, Alexei's mother sent him to find his stepfather. On his return – he had been accidentally delayed – he found her . . .

. . . sitting at the table dressed in a clean, lilac-colored frock, with her hair prettily dressed, and looking as splendid as she used to look.

"You are feeling better?" I asked, with a feeling of inexplicable fear.

Looking at me fixedly, she said:

"Come here! Where have you been? Eh?"

Before I had time to reply, she seized me by the hair, and

Alexei's only scholastic certificate, from June 8, 1879: "In approval of his outstanding progress in the sciences and good conduct, the pupil, Alexei Peshkov, has been awarded by the Elementary School of Kunavino this certificate of excellence, to serve as an example to others". As a sign of his contempt for the school, Alexei spotted the paper and added above the words "good conduct" the word "mischief", and at the lower left: "Our lousy school of Kunavino".

grasping in her other hand a long, flexible knife, made out of a saw, she flourished it several times and struck me with the flat of it. It slipped from her hands to the floor.

"Pick it up and give it to me. . . ."

I picked up the knife and threw it on the table, and mother pushed me away from her. I sat on the ledge of the stove and watched her movements in a state of terror.

Rising from the chair she slowly made her way towards her own corner, lay down on the bed, and wiped her perspiring face with a handkerchief. Her hands moved uncertainly; twice she missed her face and touched the pillow instead.

"Give me some water. . . ."

I scooped some water out of a pail with a cup, and lifting her head with difficulty, she drank a little. Then she pushed my hand away with her cold hand, and drew a deep breath. Then after looking at the corner where the icon was, she turned her eyes on me, moved her lips as if she were smiling, and slowly let her long lashes droop over her eyes. Her elbows were pressed close against her sides, and her hands, on which the fingers were weakly twitching, crept about her chest, moving towards her throat. A shadow fell upon her face, invading every part of it, staining the skin yellow, sharpening the nose. Her mouth was open as if she were amazed at something, but her breathing was not audible. I stood, for how long I do not know, by my mother's bedside, with the cup in my hand, watching her face grow frozen and gray.

When grandfather came in I said to him:

"Mother is dead."

He glanced at the bed.

"Why are you telling lies?"

He went to the stove and took out the pie, rattling the dampers deafeningly.

I looked at him, knowing that mother was dead, and waiting for him to find it out.

A few days after my mother's funeral, grandfather said to me:

"Now, Alex, you must not hang round my neck. There is no room for you here. You will have to go out into the world."

And so I went out into the world.

IN THE WORLD

Shop-boy in a boot store, Alexei – age twelve – worked laboriously in the midst of all the commotion, "weighed down with depression." He wanted to run away. By accident, he scalded his hands; he was taken to the hospital, after which he went home to his grandmother. By this time, she was forced to beg alms.

> Once more my life flowed on swiftly and full of interest, with a broad stream of impressions bringing something new to my soul every day, stirring it to enthusiasm, disturbing it, or causing me pain, but at any rate forcing me to think. . . . The earth which is ever creating gave a mighty sigh. All was coarse and naked, but it instilled a great, deep faith in that gloomy life, so shamelessly animal. At times above the noise certain painful, never-to-be-forgotten words went straight to one's heart:
>
> "It is not right for you all together to set upon one. You must take turns." "Who pities us when we do not pity ourselves?"

The burial of his little brother, the damp earth, the odor, the rotted boards uncovered by the clumsy gravedigger:

> Stiffening, I asked grandmother:
>
> "That black thing in the grave, was it mother's coffin?"

"Yes," she said angrily. "Ignorant dog! * It is not a year yet, and our Varia is already decayed!"

"Shall we all decay?"

"All. Only the saints escape it."

She halted, set my cap straight, and said to me seriously: "Don't think about it. . . . Do you hear?"

But I did think of it. How offensive and revolting death was! How odious!

Alexei was apprenticed to a designer and lived in his depressing house with the cruel family.

I had a lot of work to do. I fulfilled all the duties of a housemaid, washed the kitchen over on Wednesday, cleaning the samovar and all the copper vessels, and on Saturday cleaned the floor of the rest of the house and both staircases. I had to chop and bring in the wood for the stoves, wash up, prepare vegetables for cooking, and go marketing with the mistress, carrying her basket of purchases after her, besides running errands to the shops and to the chemist.

In his employers' home he found only smugness and wickedness. His sole refuge was the church.

They would not let me go out. . . . But they made me go to church. . . . I liked being in church. Standing somewhere in a corner where there was more room and where it was darker, I loved to gaze from a distance at the icon stand, which looked as if it were swimming in the candlelight flowing in rich, broad streams over the pulpit. The dark figures of the icons moved gently, the gold embroidery on the vestments of the priests quivered joyfully, the candle flames burned in the dark-blue atmosphere like golden bees, and the heads of the women and children looked like flowers. All the surroundings seemed to blend harmoniously with the singing choir. Everything seemed imbued with the weird spirit of legends. The church seemed to oscillate like a cradle, rocking in pitch-black space.

Sometimes, playing truant from vespers, Alexei wandered through the streets, peeping through windows, spying on peoples' lives.

---

* This to the gravedigger who had disturbed her coffin. (Trans. note.)

These walks at night beneath the winter sky through the deserted streets of the town enriched me greatly. I purposely chose streets removed from the center, where there were many lamps and friends of my master who might have recognized me.

Many and diverse were the pictures which I saw through those windows. I saw people praying, kissing, quarreling, playing cards, talking busily and soundlessly the while. It was a cheap panoramic show representing a dumb, fish-like life.

Alexei ran away. After working as cook's-boy aboard a steamboat, where the cook, Smury, had let the boy read his books, Alexei returned to his grandparents. But in the fall, his grandfather brought him back to the designer's, and there he was once again thrown "into a fog of stupefying grief." Out in the yard the people were brutish and quarrelsome.

Their attitude towards women was primitive and coarse. Willingly and unwillingly, I observed these affairs, which often went on under my eyes, beginning and ending with striking and impure swiftness.

I remember that life seemed to me to grow more and more tedious, cruel, fixed forever in those forms of it which I saw from day to day. I did not dream of anything better than that which passed interminably before my eyes.

Still, he found some people of a different nature. A little tailor's wife loaned him books, and in secret he read illustrated magazine supplements.

I have sad and ludicrous reasons for remembering the burdensome humiliations, insults, and alarms which my swiftly developed passion for reading brought me.

The books of the tailor's wife looked as if they were terribly expensive, and I was afraid that the old mistress might burn them in the stove; I tried not to think of them, and began to buy small colored books from the shop where I bought bread in the mornings.

I was not allowed to have a light, for they took the candles into the bedrooms, and I had no money to buy them for myself; so I began to collect the tallow from the candlesticks on the quiet, and put it in a sardine tin, into which I also poured lamp oil, and, making a wick with some thread, was able to make a smoky light. This I put on the stove for the night.

When I turned the pages of the great volumes, the bright red tongue of flame quivered agitatedly, the wick was drowned in the burning, evil-smelling fat, and the smoke made my eyes smart. But all this unpleasantness was swallowed up in the enjoyment with which I looked at the illustrations and read the captions. These illustrations opened up before me a world which increased daily in breadth – a world adorned with towns. . . . They showed me the lofty hills and lovely seashores. Life developed wonderfully for me. The earth became more fascinating, rich in people, abounding in towns and all kind of things.

The captions on the illustrations told me . . . about other countries, other peoples . . . but there was a lot which I did not understand, and that worried me. Sometimes strange words stuck in my brain, like "metaphysics," "chiliasm," "chartist." They were a source of great anxiety to me, and seemed to grow into monsters obstructing my vision. I thought I would never understand anything. . . . In fact, they stood like sentries on the threshold of all secret knowledge.

That Rome was a city, I knew; but who on earth were the Huns? I simply had to find out.

"The Huns," said the chemist's dispenser, Paul Goldberg, "were a nomad race like the people of Kirghiz. There are no more of these people now. They are all dead."

I felt sad and vexed, not because the Huns were dead, but because the meaning of the word that had worried me for so long was quite simple, and was also of no use to me.

But I was grateful to the Huns after my collision with the word ceased to worry me so much, and thanks to Attila, I made the acquaintance of the dispenser Goldberg.

This man knew the literal meaning of all words of wisdom. He had the keys to all knowledge.

The capsule lectures which the dispenser gave me instilled into my mind a still deeper regard for books. They gradually became as necessary to me as vodka to the drunkard.

But his employers snatched away this spiritual nourishment.

Deprived of books, I became lazy and drowsy, and became

a victim of forgetfulness, to which I had been a stranger before.

For some carelessness in a household matter, the old lady of the establishment beat Alexei so badly that it was necessary to take him to the hospital. The doctor urged him to bring a charge of assault and battery, but the boy refused to lodge a complaint. He took advantage of the effect of his noble attitude to wheedle from his employers permission to go on with his reading.

Once more I read the thick books of Dumas père, Ponson de Terraille, Montepin, Zaconne, Gaboriau, Emar and Bouagobert. I devoured all these books quickly, one after the other, and I was happy. I felt myself to be part of a life which was out of the ordinary, which stirred me sweetly and aroused my courage. Once more I burned my improvised candle, and read all through the night till the morning, so that my eyes began to hurt me a little. The old mistress said to me kindly:

"Take care, bookworm. You will spoil your sight and grow blind."

However, I soon realized that all these interestingly complicated books, despite the different incidents, and the various countries and towns about which they were written, had one common theme: good people made unhappy and oppressed by bad people; the latter were always more successful and clever than the good, but in the end, through some unexpected turn, the good ones always overcame the wicked, and emerged the victors. The "love," of which both men and women spoke in the same terms, bored me. In fact, it was not only uninteresting to me, but it aroused a vague contempt.

But through all this I saw the glimmer of living and, to me, significant truths, the outlines of another life, other standards. It was clear to me that in Paris the cabmen, working men, soldiers, and all common people were not at all as they were in Nizhni, Kazan, or Perm. They dared to speak to gentlefolk, and behaved toward them more simply and independently than our people. And in general it seemed to me that life abroad, as it appeared in books, was more interesting, easier, better than the life I knew. Abroad, people did not behave so brutally. They never jeered at other human creatures as cruelly, nor prayed to God as importunately. . . . What I noticed particularly was that, when villains, misers, and low characters were depicted in books, they did not show that incomprehensible cruelty, that inclination to jeer at humanity, with which I was acquainted, and which was often brought to my notice. There was method in the cruelty of these bookish villains. One could almost understand why they were cruel; but the cruelty which I witnessed was aimless, senseless, an amusement from which no one expected to gain any advantage.

And then there fell into my hands Goncourt's novel, *The Brothers Zemganno*. I read it through in one night, and, surprised at the new experience, read the simple, pathetic story over again. There was nothing complicated about it, nothing interesting at first sight. In fact, the first pages seemed dry, like the lives of the saints. Its language, so precise and stripped of all adornment, was at first an unpleasant surprise to me; but the paucity of words, the strongly constructed phrases, went straight to the heart. It so aptly described the drama of the acrobat brothers that my hands trembled with the enjoyment of reading the book. . . .

Soon after that I was given a "real" book, *Eugénie Grandet*. Old Grandet reminded me vividly of grandfather. I was annoyed that the book was so small, and surprised at the amount of truth it contained. Truths which were familiar and boring to me in life were shown to me in a different light in this book, without malice and quite calmly. All the books which I had read before Goncourt's condemned people as severely and noisily as my employers did, often arousing my sympathy for the villian and a feeling of irritation with the good people.

In Goncourt . . . and Balzac there were no villains, but just simple people, wonderfully alive. One could not doubt that, whatever they were alleged to have said and done, they really did say and do, and they could not have said and done anything else.

A new tenant came to live in the house, a beautiful, rich, proud young woman. She brought with her a world of which Alexei knew nothing, a world of dreams and pleasure. For the boy she was to become the distant ideal whose memory, colored with emotion, he preserved throughout his life. In his

Young Alexei's reading ranged from cloak and dagger novels to Russian classics. Second row from top, l. to r., *Queen Margot*, *Eugénie Grandet*, *A Simple Heart*, and Béranger's *Chansons*.

secret heart he named her after the most beloved heroine of his reading, "Queen Margot." It was she who was the first to have him read Pushkin's poems.

I read all of them at once, seizing upon them with a feeling of greed such as I experienced whenever I happened to visit a beautiful place that I had never seen before, in whose every corner I tried to be at once.

Pushkin had so surprised me with the simplicity and music of poetry that for a long time prose seemed unnatural to me. . . .

Then a new phase to delight Alexei: Béranger.

These songs made me feel giddy, with their strange mixture of bitter grief and boisterous happiness.

I was healthy, strong, well aware of the relations between men and women, but I saw these mysteries treated with such an incisive malice, so savage and dirty, that I was unable to picture her in the arms of a man. It was impossible for me to think that anyone would have the right to touch her boldly, lewdly, in possession of her body. I felt sure that the love of the kitchen and the pantry was unknown to Queen Margot. She knew something different, a higher joy, a different kind of love.

She continued Alexei's education, lending him the Russian classics of poetry and prose.

These books laved my soul, washing away the husks of barren and bitter reality. I felt that these were good books, and realized that they were indispensable to me. One result of reading them was that I gained a firm conviction that I was not alone in the world, and the fact that I should not be lost took root in my soul.

Books rendered many evils innocuous for me. Knowing how people loved and suffered, I could never enter a house of ill fame. Cheap depravity only roused a feeling of repulsion and pity for those to whom it was sweet.

Henry IV was nearly always the hero of the stories I told the stoker, and it seemed to me that Yaakov also loved France and "Khenrik."

Alexei became shopboy in the establishment of an icon merchant and soon went to work in the studio. This was a new world, of shrewd, ineffectual theologians, of Old Believers and sectarians.

They told stories of persecutions suffered at the hands of the official Church. . . . The words: police, search, prison, justice, Siberia – these words, continually recurring in their conversations about the persecutions for religious beliefs, fell on my heart like hot coals, kindling sympathy and fellow feeling for these Old Believers. Reading had taught me to look up to people who were obstinate in pursuing their aims. . . .

At length . . . I understood that this obstinacy was [only] . . . passivity. . . . This belief founded on habit is one of the most grievous and harmful manifestations of our lives. Within the domain of such beliefs, as within the shadows of stone walls, anything new is born slowly, is deformed, and grows anemic.

All the inhabitants of the bazaar, merchants and shopkeepers, lived a strange life, full of stupid, puerile, and always malicious diversions. . . . An unconquerable feeling of boredom oppressed them all.

After a day in the workshop, the icon painters drank heavily, sang melancholy songs, or savagely beat one another to a pulp. Always hovering over this animal existence was the radiant image of Queen Margot.

The evenings were free. I used to tell them stories about life on the steamer and different stories out of books, and without noticing how it came about, I soon held a peculiar position in the workshop as story-teller and reader.

I began to look about diligently for books, found them, and read almost every evening. Those were pleasant evenings. It was as quiet as night in the workshop; the glass balls hung over the tables like white cold stars, their rays lighting up shaggy and bald heads. I saw round me at the table, calm, thoughtful faces; now and again an exclamation of praise of the author or hero was heard. They were attentive and benign, quite unlike themselves. I liked them very much at those times, and they also behaved well to me. I felt that I was in my right place.

I began to think too much about women, and I had already revolved in my own mind the question: Shall I go on the next holiday where all the others go? This was no physical desire. I was both healthy and fastidious, but at times I was almost mad with a desire to embrace someone tender, intelligent, and frankly, unrestrainedly, as to a mother, speak to her of the disturbances of my soul.

I smoked a lot; tobacco intoxicated me, dulled my restless thoughts, my agitated feelings. As for vodka, it only aroused in me a repulsion . . .

Alexei ran into his former master, the designer-contractor, who hired him as a kind of overseer of his construction in the Nizhni market place. He spent his days among the workmen and in the evenings returned to the old house.

I returned home feeling that I was a grown man, capable of any kind of work.

I had books at home. In the flat which Queen Margot had occupied there now lived a large family – five young ladies, each one more beautiful than the other, and two schoolboys – and these people used to give me books. I read Turgenev with avidity, amazed to find how intelligible, simple, and pellucid as autumn he was; how pure were his characters, and how good everything was about which he discoursed succinctly. . . . I enjoyed reading Russian books. I always felt that there was something about them familiar and melancholy, as if there were hidden in their pages the frozen sound of the Lenten bell, which pealed forth softly as soon as one opened the book.

Dead Souls I read reluctantly; *Letters from the House of the Dead,* also. *Dead Souls, Dead Houses, Three Deaths, Living Relics* – these books with titles so much alike arrested my attention against my will, and aroused a torpid antipathy for all such books. . . . But I was delighted with Dickens and Walter Scott. I read these authors with the greatest enjoyment, the same books over and over again. The works of Walter Scott reminded me of a high mass on a great feast day in rich churches – somewhat long and tedious, but always impressive. Dickens still remains for me the author who had a wonderful grasp of that most difficult of arts – love of human nature.

In the evenings a large company of people used to gather on the roof. . . . They talked of books and poetry. This was something which appealed to me, and which I could understand; I had read more than all of them together. But sometimes they talked about the high school, and complained about the teachers. When I listened to these recitals, I felt that I had more liberty than my friends, and was amazed at their patience. And yet I envied them; they had opportunities of learning!

My comrades were older than I, but I felt that I was the elder. I was keener-witted, more experienced than they. This worried me somewhat; I wanted to feel more in touch with them. I used to get home late in the evening, dusty and dirty, steeped in impressions very different from theirs – in the main very monotonous. They talked a lot about young ladies, and of being in love with this one and that one, and they used to try their hands at writing poetry. They frequently solicited my help in this matter. I willingly applied myself to versification, and it was easy for me to find the rhymes, but for some reason or other my verses always took a humorous turn. . . .

On holidays I often wandered out of the town to "Millioni Street," * where the dockers lived. . . .

* The name was given in a spirit of mockery.

I ardently studied these people, closely packed in that old and dirty sack of a street. All of them were people who had cut themselves off from ordinary life, but they seemed to have created a life of their own, independent of any master, and gay. Careless, audacious, they reminded me of grandfather's stories about the bargemen who so easily transformed themselves into brigands or hermits. When there was no work, they were not squeamish about committing small thefts from the barges and steamers, but that did not trouble me, for I saw that life was sewn with theft, like an old coat with gray threads. At the same time I saw that these people never worked with enthusiasm, although unsparing of their energies in cases of urgency, such as fires, or the break up of ice. And, as a rule, they lived more of a holiday life than any other people.

I did not drink vodka, and I had nothing to do with girls; books took the place of these two forms of intoxication for me. But the more I read, the harder it was for me to go on living the empty, useless life that most people lived.

I had only just turned fifteen years of age, but sometimes I felt like an elderly man. I was, as it were, inwardly swollen and heavy with all I had lived through and read, or restlessly pondered. Looking into myself, I discovered that my receptacle for impressions was like a dark lumber-room closely packed with all kinds of things, of which I had neither the strength nor the wit to rid myself.

I had a fastidious dislike of unhappiness, illness, and grievances. When I saw cruelty, blood, fights, even verbal baiting of a person, it aroused a physical repulsion in me which was swiftly transformed into a cold fury. This made me fight, like a wild beast, after which I would be painfully ashamed of myself.

Within me dwelt two persons. One was cognizant of only too many abominations and obscentities, somewhat timid for that reason; this one was crushed by the knowledge of everyday horrors, and had begun to view life and people distrustfully, contemptuously, with a feeble pity for everyone, including himself. This person dreamed of a quiet, solitary life with books, without people, of monasteries, of a forest-keeper's lodge, a railway signal box, of Persia, and the office of night watchman somewhere on the outskirts of the town.

Only to see fewer people, to be remote from human creatures!

The other person, baptized by the holy spirit of noble and wise books, observing the overwhelming strength of the daily horrors of life, felt how easily that strength might sap one's brain-power, trample the heart with dirty footprints, and, fighting against it with all his force, with clenched teeth and fists, was always ready for a quarrel or a fight. He loved and pitied actively, and, like the brave hero in French novels, drew his sword from his scabbard on the slightest provocation, and assumed a fighting stance.

What went to my head most of all was the attitude of the average man toward women. From my reading of novels I had learned to look upon woman as the best and most significant thing in life.

The books of Turgenev sang the praises of woman, and together with all the good I knew about women I had enshrined the image of Queen Margot in my memory. Heine and Turgenev especially gave me much that was precious for this purpose.

In the autumn of that year I went to Kazan, in the secret hope of finding some means of studying there.

The fortress at Kazan.

MY UNIVERSITIES

This was not going to be easy. Alexei was to encounter once again misery, hard manual labor, and the impossibility of devoting himself to study.

The little house stood alone on a rise at the end of a narrow, impoverished street. One of its walls faced the ruins of a burned-out building. Weeds had sprung up thickly all over the place. From a tangle of wormwood, nettles, horse-sorrel, and elderberry bushes, rose the remains of a brick structure. I recall its large cellar where homeless dogs lived and died.

This was one of my universities. . . .

To keep from starving I went to the boat-landing on the Volga where one could earn fifteen or twenty kopeks a day. Among the longshoremen, hoboes, and drifters I felt like a piece of iron thrown into the midst of red-hot coals. Every day saturated me with a thousand burning impressions. Before me the coarse lives, naked in their greed, swirled like a tornado. Their bitterness pleased me, their jeering hostility towards the whole world and their carelessness concerning themselves. My past life drew me towards these men, arousing a desire to immerse myself in their corroding depths. Bret Harte and other fiction of adventurous outcasts helped to arouse further my sympathies for this life.

A schoolboy, Guri Pletnev . . .

Learning of the difficult and dangerous life I led, he invited me to live with him and set to work to prepare me to be a rural teacher.

And so there I was, living in the strange ebullient hole "Marussovka" . . . a large slum house on Fishmonger Street, which looked as though it had been taken by storm by the starved students, street-girls, and ghostlike men who lived there.

Pletnev worked as a newspaper proofreader, making twelve kopeks a night, and whenever I failed to earn something, we made our meals on four pounds of bread a day, two kopeks worth of tea and three of sugar. My studies left me little time for remunerative work. I mastered sciences with the greatest difficulty; grammar, with its monstrously narrow, stiff forms, oppressed me particularly. I was altogether unable to confine the living, protean, and capricious Russian language in these forms. . . .

Pletnev and I used the same cot – I, in the night – he, during the day. . . .

Alone, I explored the passages and corners of "Marussovka," observing the life of its inhabitants, a species new to me. The house swarmed like an ant heap. It was impregnated with sour, corrosive smells and in all corners were concealed heavy, menacing shadows.

There were also revolutionaries in Kazan, and Alexei found himself engaged in "conspiracy."

I was introduced to Andrei Derenkov, owner of a small grocery hidden at the end of a miserable little alley over a ditch filled with refuse.

Derenkov, a man with a withered arm, a kind face framed by a fair beard, and a pair of intelligent eyes, had the best collection of rare and prohibited books in town. He made them available to students of the numerous Kazan schools and various revolutionary-minded people. . . . Behind the kitchen, in a dark passage that joined the addition with the house, was concealed a storeroom containing the illegal library. A number of the books were handwritten copies in thick notebooks. . . . All these manuscripts were shabby and worn.

Derenkov trustingly confided to me that the modest profit of his trade went entirely for the benefit of the men who believed that "the happiness of the people goes before all else."

The real masters in the flat of the Derenkovs were the seminary and veterinary students from the university, who lived in a state of noisy solicitude as regards the Russian peasant and incessant anxiety as to the future of the country.

Of course, I understood little of those discussions, the truths were lost to me in the volume of words, like the little globules of fat in the thin soup of the poor. Some of the students reminded me of the old sectarian Bible-readers of the Volga, but I realized that these people were attempting to transform life, and, although their sincerity was smothered by the torrent of words, it did not drown in it. The questions which they tried to solve were clear to me and I felt myself personally affected by the reaching of a successful conclusion. Often my dumb thoughts seemed to ring in their words and I treated those people with the rapture of a captive promised his freedom.

They viewed me as a joiner looks at a piece of wood out of which he might make something rather uncommon.

"Unspoiled!" they would say, recommending me to each other, with the pride of street-urchins showing each other a penny found on the pavement. For some reason I did not like to be called "unspoiled" or a "son of the people"; I felt myself to be a step-son of life and often chafed at their restrictions on the development of my mind.

He bridled at the students who tried to mold his spirit their way. Then he discovered a silent, bearded man, with broad shoulders, and a head shaved like a Tartar. This was Romas, the political exile.

They called him "Khokhol," * and I think no one knew his real name except Andrei. I learned that he was just back from a ten-year exile in the district of Yakutsk. This increased my interest in him, but did not give me enough

* The name which Great-Russians used when referring to Ukrainians. (Trans. note.)

courage to make his acquaintance, although I was not afflicted with timidity or shyness and, on the contrary, suffered from an anxious curiosity, a desire to know everything as rapidly as possible. All my life, this prevented me from studying any one particular thing thoroughly. When the talk was of the people, I felt a certain lack of confidence in myself; I could not get myself to think in the same terms as the others. For them the people were an incarnation of wisdom, spiritual beauty, and kind-heartedness, a quite god-like entity, a receptacle for all things beautiful, stately, and upright. I did not know such a people. I had seen carpenters, loaders, brick-layers, I knew Jacob, Ossip, and Gregory, and here I heard of a consubstantial People, whom they put above themselves and to whose will they made themselves submissive. To me it was they who embodied beauty and strength of mind, in them I felt concentrated a will to life, the ambition to build a new world according to new canons of love for each other.

To earn a living Alexei became a baker. Again he fell into the vulgar, crude society of workmen.

But strangely enough, behind [their jeering and bragging] I heard, or imagined I heard, undertones of sadness and shame. I noticed that in the "houses of joy," where, for a rouble, one could get a woman for a whole night, my friends behaved timidly and guiltily, which seemed natural to me.... The relation of the sexes thrilled me strangely and I observed it with avid interest.

I did not myself make use of the caresses of a woman and that placed me in an unpleasant position: both the women and the men wickedly made me their butt. Very soon they stopped asking me to come with them:

"You, my boy, don't come with us!"

"It is no fun with you around."

"... It's like being watched by a priest or a father."

Though I had read many books by that time and possessed a taste for verse – I had even tried to write some myself – I used my "own" words in speech. My words felt leaden and harsh, but it seemed to me that only with them could I express the intricate web of my thoughts.

Sometimes the coarseness was intentional out of a feeling

of rebellion against something alien in me, something aggravating. One of my teachers – a student of mathematics – reproached me:

"How queerly you speak! You don't use words, you use sash-weights!"

On the whole, I did not care for myself, as often happens with adolescents. I thoughts of myself as clumsy and coarse. I disliked my face – with the high Kalmuk cheek-bones – and my voice, which did not obey me.

. . . . on a mournful autumn night I felt for the first time the weariness of my soul and the corrosive mold over my heart. And from that hour I began to suffer badly, looking at myself with a cold, sidelong, strange, and hostile glance.

Around me life got still more grim. The students' rioting was beginning – I could not grasp its sense, it was unclear to me. I perceived in it a gay bustle, but the drama of it escaped me. It seemed to me that in return for the joy of studying at the university one could bear anything. Had anyone proposed to me: "Now, go and study, but in return, every Sunday on the Nikolai Square, we will thrash you with clubs!" I would readily have accepted this condition.

In December I decided to commit suicide. I have tried to describe the motives for this decision in the story: "An Incident in the Life of Makar." But my attempt was not successful – the story turned out awkward, unpleasing, and lacked inner truth. One of its merits is, so I think, the absolute lack of truth in it. The facts are truthful, but they look as though they were told by some one else and as though the whole story were not about me. Except for the form, I am pleased with the story; as if I had stepped outside myself.

I bought the revolver from a regimental drummer. I found it loaded with four cartridges and shot at my chest, thinking to strike the heart, but only succeeded in perforating a lung, and in a month, feeling very ashamed and foolish I was again working in the bakery.

Gorky had left a note worded as follows:

For my death I wish to blame the German poet Heine, who invented heartache. Herewith is attached my passport, expecially re-registered for this occasion. I want an autopsy to be performed on my remains so that the world may learn what sort of devil inhabited me lately. From the attached passport it is evident that I am A. Peshkov and from the rest of the note I hope nothing is evident. I am of sound mind and memory.

A. PESHKOV

Following this attempted suicide, Gorky told in another work . . .

In 1887, in Kazan, I appeared before a "spiritual" church tribunal, composed of a monk, a priest, and the archpriest of the Maslov Cathedral; I was judged according to Article 14 of the ruling of Saint Timothy, Bishop of Alexandria. I was condemned to serve penance in the Feodor Monastery, I believe, in what I form I no longer know. I refused to submit to the decision. So the monk, a little old man with green eyes, threatening and opinionated, undertook to show me that I was a thief; that I had tried to steal my life which belonged to the Czar – my master on earth – and to deliver my soul which belonged to God – my father in heaven – to Satan, his enemy. I answered that I considered myself alone the rightful master of my life and my soul. (1927)

Afterwards, Gorky returned to this attempted suicide repeatedly, always with the intention of instructing, in order to condemn the "senseless humiliation suffered" on that account. And so he said to the workers:

Comrades, I have experienced fear of life's cruelty and harshness, so much so that I tried to do away with myself. For many long years I was to remember it as a stupidity, feeling bitter shame and contempt for myself. *(How I Became a Writer*, 1928.)

Alexei was in a state of profound confusion when Romas took him along some 30 miles down the Volga, to the village of Krasnovidovo, where he had organized a revolutionary center under cover of a small business.

"You are gifted, stubborn by nature and, as it seems, with the best of aspirations. You must learn, but it must not be in such a way that books shut you off from people."

We talked until midnight, for he evidently wished to win me immediately and firmly to his side. It was the first time that I felt so tranquil with a man. After my suicide attempt,

Alexei sets out on foot across Russia (from the film *University Life*).

my self-esteem had suffered considerably, I felt myself to be a nobody, I had a guilty conscience and I was ashamed to live. I think Romas understood this and in a simple, human way invited me into his own life. And by doing so – straightened me out. It was an unforgettable day!

This turned out to be the best of Alexei's "universities." He joined with Romas in his efforts to awaken the peasants to a sentient life and to shield them from exploitation by the kulaks. But the peasants did not understand. They hated Romas and Alexei and their few partisans, and finally set fire to their co-operative. Alexei was twenty years old. He worked as a barge-man, sailed down the Volga and joined a collective of some Kalmuk fishermen on the Caspian.

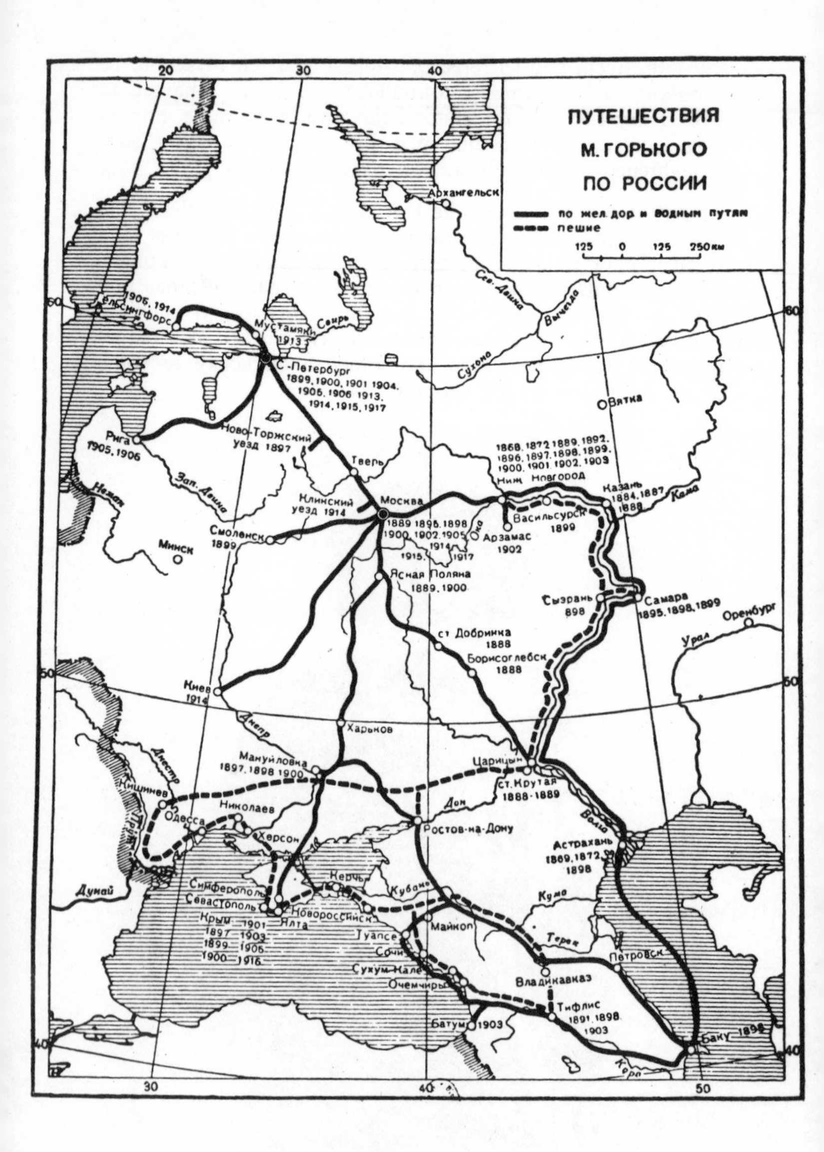

Itinerary of Gorky's journeys.
(Broken lines indicate trips made on foot).

TRAVELS

Alone, traveling through Russia, Alexei worked here and there. And so he was a railroad man, a night watchman, a weigh-man, and a gang worker. He went from one railway station to the next, living in an atmosphere of crudeness and violence, always reading and thinking.

> I poked into everything, without sparing myself, and learned much that perhaps it would have been better for me not to know, but that it is necessary to tell people, yes, necessary, for it is their life, the harsh filthy drama of the struggle between man and beast, man's attempts to conquer the elements within and outside himself. If there is anything on earth really noble an great it is the incessant growth of man, valuable even when he is hateful.

Transferred to another station, he found, at last, people of a different type.

> There I got acquainted with a considerable group of the "intelligentsia." Nearly all were "unreliable," had tasted prison and exile, had read a lot, knew foreign languages – there were expelled students, theologians, statisticians, a naval officer, and two army officers.

I walked midway between the original town people and these curious "culture bearers," and it amused me to see the incompatibility of these groups.

My youth and ignorance did not prevent me from an anguished perception of the possibility of vulgar and confused drama hidden behind the "holy prose."

Dreaming of great heroic deeds and brilliant joys, I guarded the tarpaulins and bags, the logs, sleepers, and other equipment against the Cossacks of the neighboring station. I used to read Shakespeare and Heine and then, suddenly aware of the putrefying reality around me, I would fall into a stupor for hours, doing nothing, incapable of understanding anything, as though stunned by a blow on the head.

After all that I had seen, the enlightened "intelligentsia" seemed to me drab and colorless; it seemed to flow outside that delirious, hectic bustle that formed the diseased reality of general everyday life. The more attentively I watched, the more uneasy and anxious I became.

I lacked the brains, the imagination, and the energy to join together those two worlds – separated by a deep ingrained split.

A worried perception of the moral alienation of the "intelligentsia," that is the schism between the intellectual and the popular, has persistently troubled me all my life. In my literary works I often broached this topic. . . . Gradually this perception grew into the presentiment of doom. In 1905, imprisoned in the Peter and Paul fortress, I tried to develop this point in my unsuccessful play, *Children of Sun*. If the split between reason and will is a drama in the life of an individual, it is a tragedy in the life of the people.

I was a healthy lad and possessed of an unusual strength. Nine times, without hurrying, I could cross myself with an eighty-pound weight in my hand; I easily carried sacks of flour weighing two hundred pounds – but at that hour I felt myself quite spent and weak, like a sick child. I wanted to cry from a feeling of bitter offense. I had sought avidly for a communion with the beauty of life of which the books I had read spoke so temptingly. I was ready to devote rapturous admiration to anything that would imbue me with strength to live. The time had come for me to experience the joys of life, for I felt oftener and oftener the flow of fury. It rose in a dark and hot wave to my breast, blinding my reason; it transformed my eager interest in people into a feeling of repulsion and contempt. It was painfully annoying to encounter, over and over again, things foul and stupid, pathetic and alien.

Having organized a community which aimed at a rural life, Alexei was sent by his comrades to Yasnaya Polyana to seek the aid and counsel of Tolstoy. Not finding him there, he pushed on to Moscow.

A part of the way – in the night – I used to travel with conductors of goods-trains on the platforms of the freight cars; the greater part I walked on foot, earning my bread by working in Cossack villages, on farms, and in monasteries. I roamed over the Don steppes, in the districts of Tambor and Ryazan – from Ryazan along the Oka; then I turned off to Moscow, and on my way decided to visit Tolstoy in Khamorniki, but at my arrival there Sofia Andreyevna informed me that he had gone to the Troitzo-Sergiersk monastery. I met her in the courtyard, at the door of a hut filled to the brim with books; she led me into the kitchen, kindly offering me coffee and a roll. Among other things, she told me that Tolstoy was perpetually surrounded by crowds of ne'er-do-wells and that Russia had altogether too many of that kind of people. I had had that impression myself by that time, and with an easy heart politely confirmed this clever woman's observation as being perfectly correct.

At the end of 1889, Alexei decided to approach Korolenko. The author of *The Blind Musician*, back from exile, was living in Nizhni under police scrutiny. Alexei submitted his "Song of the Old Oak," a sort of poem in prose.

I never suffered from conceit and at that time I believed myself to be an ignoramus, but I was sincerely confident that I had written an uncommonly fine thing. I had crammed it with every idea that had got into my head during the ten years of my hard and varied life and I was sure that the whole reading public, after having acquainted itself with my poem, would acclaim it for its originality. I felt sure that the truth of my story would open the hearts of all and usher in an honest, pure, and joyful life. I did not expect or desire anything more than that.

Korolenko gave the beginner his first lesson in writing. It was severe.

> I went away and spent the next few days in a state of absolute depression.
>
> Korolenko had been the first to address to me some weighty human words on the importance of structure, on the beauty of a sentence, and I was surprised at the simplicity and aptness of these words. Listening to him, I realized with a certain pang that writing was no easy task. I sat with him for more than two hours; he told me a lot, but not a word on the essence, on the content of my poem. And I knew already that the judgment on that would be unfavorable.

Nothing was working out, neither literature nor his love life. Alexei decided to set out again across Russia. He traveled for two years in the south, from the Danube to the Caspian. He brought back rich material which he was to use in his stories years later, between 1912 and 1917. Concerning this, he wrote to the editor-in-chief of *European Messenger* (Vestnik Ievropy) in which they were to appear:

> I don't know what title to give to the studies that I have sent you. I had the impertinent intention of giving them as a title: "Russia. Impressions of a man who is passing by." But wouldn't that be a little too pretentious?
>
> I say "of a man who is passing by" and not "of a passer-by." It seems to me that a passerby is vague, passive, leaves nothing of himself and carries away nothing, while the man who is passing by is, to a certain extent, an active being who gathers impressions and knowingly extracts from them a precise image. . . .
>
> It was my idea to write a series of essays of this sort. I wanted to sketch psychological characteristics and to show various aspects of the spiritual condition of Russian men, as I had grasped them.

After two years of roaming, plus a stay in Tiflis where his first novel was published, he returned to Nizhni in the autumn of 1892. He was no longer alone; a woman had entered his life.

In all the days of my life I had seen women working like slaves, living in filth and depravity, in misery or in smug and vulgar satiety. Only one beautiful memory remained from my childhood, "Queen Margot," but a whole chain of other impressions separated me from this. I thought that the story of Isergil would be appreciated by women, would excite in them the desire for beauty and freedom. But it had failed to move the woman who was the nearest of all to me – she had fallen asleep over it!

Why? Did the bell which life had cast in my breast lack resonance?

I had taken this woman into my heart, in the place of a mother. I had looked to her to nourish me with rich honey, which would rouse my creative power; I expected her to soften the brutality which had been instilled in me by life.

That was thirty years ago and I recall it now with a smile in my heart. But at that time, the indisputable right of a human being to sleep whenever he or she likes had caused me to suffer intensely.

Nizhni Novgorod in the nineteenth century.

In Nizhni, Gorky led the taxing existence of a journalist paid by the line. Many years later he drew a picture of himself during those difficult times, making a mistake in the date, by the way; at the time he was not twenty-one but twenty-four.

> I am twenty-one years old. I feel ill at ease and precarious on the earth. Like a wagon overloaded with all sorts of junk and drawn by an invisible force along an unknown path, I expect to be overturned at every crossroad.
>
> I am greatly and stubbornly preoccupied with myself, trying to gain as solid a footing as possible among the offensive, absurd contradictions which attack me from all sides, hammering at me, sometimes throwing me into a morbid state close to insanity. About a year and a half ago, I felt so weary of this agitation that I attempted suicide. With an ugly, heavy revolver, I put a bullet through my chest. Following this loathsome and stupid travesty, I felt distrust, almost contempt for myself.
>
> At present I am living in a cabin overhanging a filthy ravine, in the garden of a drunken priest. This cabin served formerly as a bath-house. A putrid odor of soap and rotting mops poisons the blood. The two rooms are freezing. Even the mice suffer from the cold and are uneasy; at night they clamber onto my bed.
>
> The cabin is overgrown with thick bushes of wild raspberries. In bad weather their clinging shoots tap at the windows and scrape the twisted, blackened planks of the walls. I live poorly, like a recluse, feeding on vague dreams of another life of brightness and ease, of chivalrous loves, of lofty deeds full of self-sacrifice. In the miserable little local newspaper I publish unintelligible stories. I am sure that I'm wrong to publish them, sure of offending the very literature which I love passionately, like a woman. Nevertheless, they are published, because I have to eat.

He recalls himself at a party with the local intelligentsia.

> I don't know how to move with the agility or the adroitness of the others; my long gnarled body is astonishingly clumsy, my arms are my enemies, they are always catching on someone or something. I am especially afraid of women and this fear adds to my awkwardness; I thump the poor ladies with

my elbows, my knees, my shoulders. My face reflects my every thought; this is extremely unfortunate. In order to hide this defect I screw up my nose and make faces. In general, I am in the way among well brought up people.

What's more, I always have the desire to talk to them about what I know of another way of life which, in a particularly malignant way, resembles theirs while being quite distinct from it. But my narrations are coarse, blundering. How out of place I feel at Chamov's Saturdays.

But his reports and short stories brought notoriety and then success. Gorky's letters to Chekhov inform us best about the writer's state of mind at the time when he was just becoming known. In them, this infintely modest man wrote all the more intimately as he had never seen Chekhov. Yet, he was deeply attached to him. For his part, Chekhov was undoubtedly the man who best understood Gorky, and Gorky's letters help us to understand him. Chekhov, a tubercular, was living in Yalta. Gorky – this was characteristic – rarely dated his letters. His biographers have established their approximate chronology.

Nizhni Novgorod, November, 1898

Please don't take it amiss if I express myself awkwardly. I'm a coarse, absurd person and my soul is mortally ill. As we know, this is befitting the soul of a person who thinks.

And since he invited the older writer's counsel, Chekhov, with exquisite delicacy, censured his lack of restraint and grace, his brutality, and his commonplace, romantic language.

Nizhni Novgorod, December, 1898

How well you wrote to me, Anton Pavlovitch; it was just what I deserved. You're right about the affected words. I am without success in banishing them from my vocabulary, and what holds me back is the fear of tumbling into vulgarity. Briefly, I am always rushed, without knowing why; I end my stories badly, and the worst is that I live exclusively by my literary earnings. There's nothing else I know how to do.

I am self-educated and thirty years old. I doubt that I shall become any better than I am – may God let me hold on to the level I have attained; it isn't very high, but it will do for me. I am not an unusual character.

But you, that's something else again, your talent is wonderfully powerful. . . .

Autumn, 1899. Gorky's success increased. He took himself to Petersburg at his publishers' call. Here is how, many years later, he was to describe his first stay in the capital. (It was really 1899; Gorky was careless about the dates in his life.):

In 1901 I came for the first to Petersburg, the town of straight lines and crooked-minded people. I was "the fashion"; "glory" besieged me, interfering with my life. . . . Of course it was very pleasant to see the kind smiles of the women, the adoring glances of the young girls and, probably like all young people, winged with glory, I rather resembled an Indian cock.

But in the nights, when I was alone, I suddenly felt myself like an escaped criminal . . . whose admission of guilt is awaited by all. . . .

Often I had to stand as a schoolboy who is being examined in all matters of science.

"What do you believe in?" questioned the sectarians and the priests of the temples. Being of an amiable disposition, I allowed myself to be examined with a patience which amazed me, but after this torture of words I experienced the desire to poke the needle of the Admiralty through Isaac's Cathedral or do something equally scandalous. Somewhere, behind a certain good nature, nearly always an affected one, Russians conceal something slightly resembling bounderism. This quality – or is it perhaps a means of investigation? – expresses itself very variedly, chiefly though in an aspiration to visit the soul of your neighbor as one visits a fair, watch the conjuring tricks that are being exhibited in it, throw things about in it and trample them, sow trifles in a stranger's soul and sometimes overturn something in it. And, like doubting Thomas, poke one's fingers in the wounds, presuming most probably that the skepticism of the Apostle is equal to the curiosity of monkeys.

And here is his literary credo:

To Chekhov, Nizhni Novgorod, January, 1900

I am leading as usual a ridiculous life, I feel wildly excited

. . . I have read your *Lady*. Do you know what you are doing? You are killing realism. Soon you will finish it, for a long time. Realism has had its day – that's a fact. Nobody knows how to go further in this direction than you, nobody is able to set down with such simplicity that which is simple. After the least of your stories, anything else seems gross, written not with a pen but a club. Most of all, everything seems to lack simplicity, that is, truth. That's right! . . . Hence, you are murdering realism and I am extremely glad. That'll do! Dammit!

I swear, our time thirsts for heroism. Everyone is calling for excitement, color; something, you see, which does not resemble life, but is above it, better, more beautiful. It is absolutely essential that today's literature improve on life, and once it begins to do so, life will appear more beautiful, men will be more animated, more alive. But now, just look at them, what unpleasant eyes they have, uninteresting, dim and frozen.

THE WRITER AND HIS PUBLIC

Back from Petersburg, Gorky wrote a pamphlet *About a Writer Who Became Conceited.* Inspired by the devil, a successful author ponders on those who over-praise him – and selects his public.

> It is not good for a writer to have many fans. Men who have anything to do with the "public" must disinfect the atmosphere with the help of the acid of truth.

These admirers are not the people . . .

> who are still ready to trade any of the arts for a bag of wheat, but the well-mannered heirs of Judas Iscariot, Ignatius Loyola, and all those who have sold Christ.
>
> "Gentlemen," [says the author] "I believe in your sincerity, only it is difficult for me to understand how I have succeeded in arousing such a response. At times, I must admit, it seems to me that you like me because I do not wear a frock-coat, and because in my stories I frequently use coarse language. . . . The real reader knows that the man who does the writing is of no importance, that only his mind counts, and he doesn't

1900

Moscow, 1903.

Portrait by Serov (1904).

inspect him like some two-headed freak. He reads without any preconceived belief but, free, he reflects and says, 'This is so. That's not so.' Having reflected, he acts, and his act becomes history. But you, gentlemen, you do not make history, but scandal. There are very few true readers on the whole earth, and you, you are not readers but the mob.

"How many real men are there among you? Perhaps there will be five out of a thousand who believe passionately that man is the creator and the master of life, and that his right to think, to speak, to move freely is a sacred right. Perhaps only five out of a thousand are capable of fighting for this right and of dying in the fight without a whimper. The majority of you are the slaves of life or its cynical patrons, and all, all of you, are meek petty bourgeois who are temporarily holding the place of real men. Your resemblance to human beings is only anatomical. I look at your lifeless cowards' eyes and I see with distress that few are daring and few are honest! How poor in brave men is my country, yet the hour is coming when it will need heroes.

"A real man, a man who is alive, is always seeking something, but you, you go along untroubled, docile, immobile, as you have been ordered to do. You lead narrow lives, too lazy to think, too frightened to stir. . . . When the open wind carries new and fresh odors into the mustiness of your burrows, you shut your windows for fear of catching cold in your souls. You don't like being disturbed, you are afraid of being disturbed! But because you need something to fill up your conversation, to entertain your guests, you hold out your hands to literature like beggars in the church square.

"Life is the heroic poem of the man who searches for his soul without finding it, who wants to know everything but never succeeds, who aspires to be strong and never manages to conquer his weakness. . . . But you, you are only eager to be satisfied, to live where it's warm, to violate and debauch women under the colors of love; your pleasure is to live smoothly, snugly, and quietly.

"Oh, how you love to be miserable! I think you do it deliberately; there's nothing about you worthy of arousing respect or love, and therefore, you make yourselves unhappy on purpose in order to provoke pity and sympathy: cheap illusions!"

The writer has chosen his public; he has entered into war against the "spineless democratic intelligentsia" whose mentality he was to put to shame. The definition of the latter was to come in his famous *Notes on the Petty Bourgeois Mentality* (1905).

The ugliest forms of the philistine attitude in regard to the people are rampant in our ridiculous country. There is probably no other nation where the ruling classes speak and write so much and so regularly concerning the people, no more than there is another literature which has shown it in such a sugar-coated form, which has described its sufferings with such a strange and suspicious pleasure.

When a man is tortured and keeps silent, firm and manly, full of contempt for his executioners, it is beautiful; one admires, one respects this martyr, and unquestionably, there is a splendid theme for a poet. . . . But when one smashes the face of the Russian *muzhik* who has most probably committed no crime; when he is whipped, when his ribs are broken and he wails, "I won't do it any more!" that isn't beautiful, that's hardly human. It ought to make the power that oppresses the people odious and detestable, and ought to stir up a passionate, stabbing desire to destroy the dreadful and stifling barracks in which our country is choking.

With feeble compassion Russian literature records how a power led astray by its impunity is doing violence to the Russian people; how that power through superstition is painstakingly devitalizing that eternal source of energy which is wrongfully turned to stone by anyone; and how the earth which gives us bread and flowers is becoming exhausted. Russian literature notes this crime against the life of its country and utters a lyric sigh:

Native land, land of long-suffering,
Land of the Russian people!

Our literature is a continual hymn to the patience of Russian men, it is saturated with a quiet ecstasy in the face of the dear little *muzhik*-martyr and stands gaping in admiration of his superhuman endurance. . . .

All the same, one senses in the attitude of the Russian writer towards his *muzhik*-heroes, a sort of satisfaction at seeing them so worthless, so spineless, so good, so patient. . . . Wittingly or not, our aristocratic literature has persisted in painting the people as passively indifferent to their living conditions, dreaming about God and their souls, wishing only for eternal peace, full of petty-bourgeois distrust of anything new, characterized by a revolting mildness, ready to forgive anything and anybody, flat-nosed idealists, capable of endless submission to all those who might wish it. . . .

Tolstoy and Dostoevsky, two geniuses among the greats, have overwhelmed the whole world with the power of their work. They have focused on Russia the amazed attention of Europe. As equals, they are ranked among the illustrious such as Shakespeare, Dante, Cervantes, Rousseau, and Goethe. But they have served their obscure, unhappy country poorly.

At exactly the time when reaction was at its height, when the best people were being overcome, Dostoevsky, instead of animating his country with the spirit of resistance, cries to the Russian people (in his speech at the unveiling of Pushkin's monument), "Endure!"

Tolstoy says, "Perfect yourself!" And he adds, "Do not resist evil with violence!"

There is in this exhortation to resignation and nonresistance to evil something oppressive, ugly, shameful, something which borders on slander. So, two universal geniuses lived in a country where oppression had reached a level of sadistic cynicism. The despotism of a power drunk with irresponsibility had transformed the entire country into one dreadful prison whose officials, from the governor down to the policeman, boldly plundered and tortured millions of men, toying with them, like a cat with a mouse.

I hear the idolators crying, "What? Tolstoy? Dostoevsky?"

I am not writing a critique on the works of these great artists, I confine myself to exposing their philistinism. Life has no worse enemies, for they wish to reconcile the executioner and the victim, in justifying their friendship with the executioners and their apathy before the sufferings of the world. . . .

This is a monstrous thing.

GORKY AGAINST THE WEST

After having played a vital part in the revolution of 1905, Gorky, hunted by the Czarist police, fled Russia in the early days of 1906. His arrival in France coincided with the Petersburg government's campaign to negotiate a loan from the western powers. Gorky conducted an active propaganda against this loan. When the French financiers, backed by the government, agreed to the loan, Gorky brought out in the summer of 1906 a bitter pamphlet called, "*La Belle France.*"

The author walked the streets of Paris a long time looking for "*la belle France.*" He finally found her in her cheerless abode: a police station near the Alexander III Bridge.

> Near the door through which I entered stood two soldiers clad in pants made of the Red Flag of Liberty. There were the remains of an inscription over the entrance, of which one could only make out: "Lib...Equ...Fra...ty." This brought to mind the gang of bankers who had disgraced the land of Béranger and George Sand. The atmosphere was laden with the stench of mold, decay and corruption.
>
> My heart beat violently. Like all revolutionaries, I too in my youth had loved this woman, who herself knew how to love sincerely and generously, and to make revolutions beautifully. . . .
>
> The walls were papered with vari-colored Russian loan bonds, and the floor was covered with the skins of colonial natives on which the words of the "Declaration of the Rights of Man" were artistically chased. The furniture, made of

the bones of men who had died on the barricades . . . was upholstered with a dark material on which was embroidered the treaty of alliance with the Russian Czar. On the walls hung the coats of arms of European states . . .: the mailed fist of Germany, the noose and knout of Russia, the beggar's pouch of Italy, and the arms of Spain – the black cassock of a Catholic priest and his bony hands greedily clutching the neck of a Spaniard. There was also the emblem of France: the portly stomach of a bourgeois, with a masticated Phrygian cap inside it. . . .

[*La belle France*] entered and through her drooping eyelashes swiftly scrutinized me with the glance of a connoisseur of men.

"You speak French?" she inquired, responding to my bow with the gesture of an actress who had long ceased to play queenly roles.

"No, madam, I speak only the truth," I replied.

After a conversation "with this cowardly cynical cocotte," the writer left.

I walked the streets of Paris and my heart sang a hymn to the France with whom I had talked in the dark cell.

Who in the dawn of his days has not loved thee with all his heart?

In the years of youth, when the soul of man kneels in worship before the Goddesses of Beauty and Liberty, the heart saw their bright shrine in none but thee, O great France!

France! To all honest and courageous men that dear word sounded like the precious name of a passionately beloved bride. How numerous were the great days in thy past! Thy battles were bright festivals for the peoples, and from thy sufferings they drew supreme lessons.

France! The belfry of the world, from whose summit three strokes of the bell of justice once resounded through the earth, three cries that awakened people from their prolonged slumber – Liberty, Equality, Fraternity!

And now . . .

All thy finest children are against thee . . . mistress of bankers. . . .

And thou, mother of Liberty, thou, Joan of Arc, hast

given strength to brute beasts that they may seek again to crush the people.

Great France, once the cultural leader of the world, dost thou realize the utter abomination of thy deeds?

Thy venal hand has for a time barred the road of liberty and culture to a whole nation. And even if that time be only one day, thy crime will be none the less.

My beloved!

I spit a gout of blood and gall in thine eyes!

Indignant, some French journalists showered reproaches on him. He learned of their abuse only on his return to France from the United States, at which time he responded with two letters in *l'Humanité* of December 11. The letters were entitled: "To My Detractors." The first, in a subdued tone, was addressed to the historian Aulard, whose signature Gorky had read "with surprise and regret!"

Your book on the epic struggle of the French people against tyranny is read by the Russian proletariat, which learns from it how to make sacrifices and how to perish for freedom, which is as necessary to it as air.

Without this accursed money there would not have been so much fierce blood-letting of the Russsian people. And whether you like it or not, this treacherous loan has caused the face of the bourgeoisie and the French government to be stained shamefully with Russian blood. . . .

You are mistaken also when you suppose that I aimed my invective against all France. Why do you think me so naive? I know the people are never responsible for the politics of the ruling classes or their faithful lackey, the government. In particular, I know the French, who have sown the seeds of liberty throughout Europe, and I know they would not act against liberty had they full knowledge of the facts. But, as usual, the people are tricked and dishonored by the masters of their existence, and it is to them, be they German, English, French, kings, bankers, or traitorous journalists, that I direct my curses.

I was speaking to the France of the bankers and financiers, to the France of the police and the ministries. I spit in the face of that France which decried Émile Zola.

The Russian revolution will grow slowly and for a long time, but it will end in the victory of the people. . . . When power and authority are in the hands of the people, they will be reminded of the French bankers who helped the Romanov family to fight against the freedom of justice and truth and to retain their rule, whose barbarian and anti-cultural role is clearly seen and felt by all the honest . . . hearts in [France].

And he closed with these prophetic words:

I am certain that the Russian people will not return to France the loans already repaid with their blood. They will not!

The second letter, in a much more savage tone, was addressed to Messieurs Gérault-Richard, René Viviani, Jules Claretie and other French journalists.

I have acquainted myself with the fountains of eloquence that gushed from your inkwells, prompted by my article on the loan. . . . I don't congratulate you!

Alliance with the so-called Russian government is doing you good: you have begun to treat logic, truth, and the noble French language in exactly the way Cossacks treat women. One reason, you see, why tyranny is so atrocious is that it perverts even the unconcerned and indifferent onlooker, which is what has happened to you.

I never reply to personal attacks, and the ruder they are, the sooner they are forgotten. But, sirs, you accuse me of ingratitude – and that I cannot let pass.

You say: "we came out in Gorky's defense when he was in prison, yet he. . . ."

I take the liberty of giving you a piece of good advice: If, whether from inadvertence or for some other reason, you once allowed free play to your humane sentiments, don't brag about it! It isn't nice. . . .

"I was good to you, you should repay me with gratitude" – that is what is to be gathered from your words. But I don't feel grateful, and I consider your kindness a misunderstanding.

I am not the martyr or sufferer you would so zealously make me out to be. I am just a man who confidently does his small job and finds complete satisfaction in his work, and if for this I have sometimes been put in jail for brief periods – well, I just rested there from natural fatigue,

In the United States,
1906.

without experiencing any particular discomfort, let alone suffering.

From the standpoint of common sense, you, sirs, ought to wish that I be put in prison more often and for longer periods, and when you protest against it, I find your conduct – forgive me! – just funny.

For we are enemies, and implacable enemies, I am certain. An honest writer is always an enemy of society, and even more an enemy of those who defend and justify greed and envy, those basic pillars of the modern social organization.

You also say: "We love Gorky, yet he. . . ."

Sirs, let me tell you quite sincerely: to me, a socialist, the love of a bourgeois is profoundly offensive!

I trust that these lines will define our mutual relations accurately and for all time.

Gorky went to the United States in the capacity of a revolutionary propagandist, with the same purpose of stirring up public opinion against any financial aid to the Czar's government. The latter alerted its ambassador in New York so that he might thwart this activity. The ambassador only succeeded in unleashing against Gorky American prudery, when he revealed that Madame Maria Andreyeva, who accompanied him, was not his legal wife. The hotels closed their doors to the couple. Gorky was to write later . . .

. . . a modest scandal staged by pious Americans. I had been driven out of two hotels. So I planted myself with my trunks in the street, and I decided to wait and see what would happen. I was surrounded by reporters, about fifteen of them. In their own American way, they were good fellows. They "sympathized" with me, and were even, I thought, rather embarrassed by the scandal. One of them . . . guessed that I was quite willing to let the scandal take its course. He persuaded the young writer Leroy Scott and his comrades to "take a hand in the affair." . . . I was removed from the street to the "club" – an apartment where five writers lived in a "commune," and where Scott's wife, a Russian Jewess, was the housewife. The young writers used to gather in the evening in front of the fireplace in the "club's" spacious vestibule. Reporters came, and I talked to them about literature, the Russian revolution, the Moscow insurrection (N. E. Burenin, member of the military organization of the

Bolshevik Central Committee, Scott's wife, and M. F. Andreyeva translated what I said into English). The newspapermen listened, took notes, and, with a sigh of evident regret, said:

"It's all devilishly interesting – but it's not for our papers." *(The Bourgeois Press)*

Gorky drew inspiration from this scandal for a passage in his imaginary interview with an American multi-millionaire. It was published in a series of bitter pamphlets against the United States. The magnate declared:

> It is impossible for an American to recognize Christ! . . . He was born out of wedlock! . . . A man born out of wedlock cannot even be an official in America to say nothing of a god. He is not received anywhere in decent society. Not a single girl will agree to marry him. Oh, we are very strict! And if we were to recognize Christ, we would also have to accept all the illegitimately born as respectable people . . . even if they were born of a Negro and a white woman. Think how horrible that would be! *(One of the Kings of the Republic)*

Falsehood
Racism
Cosmopolitism
Incitement
Militarism
Obscurantism
Calumny
Fascism

The bourgeoisie is the enemy of culture
M. GORKY.

This is the "spirit" of the contemporary bourgeoisie, of its culture; an abominable, shameful spirit.
M. GORKY.

With Lenin.

GORKY AND LENIN

Gorky met Lenin in London in May, 1907, during the Fifth Congress of the Russian Social-Democratic Labor Party.

Before me now stood a baldheaded, stocky, sturdy person, . . . holding my hand in one of his, while with the other he wiped a forehead which might have belonged to Socrates, beaming affectionately at me with his strangely bright eyes.

He began at once to speak about the defects of my book *The Mother* – evidently he had read it in manuscript. . . . I was hurrying to finish the book, I said – but did not succeed in saying why. Lenin with a nod of assent, himself gave the explanation: Yes, I should hurry up with it, such a book is needed, for many of the workers who take part in the revolutionary movement do so unconsciously and chaotically, and it would be very useful to them to read *The Mother*. "The very book for the moment." This was the single compliment he paid me, but it was a most precious one to me.

Then he went on to ask in a businesslike way, if it was being translated, whether it had been mangled much by the Russian and American censorship. When I told him that the author was to prosecuted, at first he frowned, then threw back his head, closed his eyes and burst into unusual laughter.

He seemed to me to speak badly, but after a minute [when he had taken the floor] I and everybody else were absorbed in his speech. It was the first time I had heard complicated political questions treated so simply. There was no striving after eloquent phrases with him, but every word was uttered distinctly, and its meaning marvelously plain. It is very difficult to pass on to the reader the unusual impression which he made.

I briefly related my adventures [in America]. I have never met a man who could laugh so infectiously as Lenin. It was strange to see such a stern realist, a man who saw so well, and felt so deeply, the inevitability of great social catastrophes, irreconcilable, relentless in his hatred towards the capitalist world, laughing like a child, till the tears came, till he choked with laughter. To laugh like that one must have the soundest and healthiest of minds.

"Oh, you are a – humorist!" he said through his laughter. "I would never have thought that anything could be so funny."

Wiping his eyes, he was at once serious, and said with his kind, soft smile: "It's a good thing that you can meet failure with humor. Humor is a splendid, healthy quality. And really life is as funny as it is sad, just as much."

I cannot imagine another man who, so far surpasssing other people, could yet remain unaffected by ambitious cravings and retain a lively interest in simple folk.

There was a certain magnetic quality in him which drew the hearts and sympathies of the working people to him.

Life plays such malicious tricks on us, that those who are incapable of real hatred are incapable of real love also. This fact alone, distorting human nature at the root, this unavoidable division of the soul, the inevitability of love through hatred, condemns modern conditions of life to dissolution.

I have never met in Russia, the country where the inevitability of suffering is preached as the general road to salvation, nor do I know of any man, who hated, loathed, and despised so deeply and strongly as Lenin all unhappiness, grief and suffering. . . . The literature of Russia is the most pessimistic in Europe. All our books are written on one and the same theme – how we suffer in youth and middle-age from our own foolishness, from the oppressive weight of autocracy, on account of woman, from love of one's neighbor, from the unsuccessful structure of the universe; how we suffer in old age from consciousness of the mistakes we have made in our lives, from lack of teeth, from indigestion and the imminence of death. Every Russian who has passed a month in prison for some political offense, and a year in exile, considers it his sacred duty to present Russia with a book of reminiscences about his sufferings. But a happy life no one has ever thought of putting into the form of memoirs. As Russians are in the habit of thinking out what their lives shall be, but unable to make them come out that way, maybe such a book would teach them how to devise a happy life.

Lenin was exceptionally great, in my opinion, precisely because of this feeling in him of irreconcilable, unquenchable hostility towards the sufferings of humanity, his burning faith that suffering is not an essential and unavoidable part of life, but an abomination which people ought and are able to sweep away. I should define this fundamental character trait as the militant optimism of a materialist. It is this trait which attracted me the most to this man – Man with a capital.

In the years 1917-18 my relations with Lenin were not what I would have wished them to be, but they could not be otherwise. He was a politician. He had to perfection that clear-sighted directness of vision which is so indispensable in the helmsman of so enormous and heavily burdened a ship as Russia with its dead-weight of peasants. I have an organic distaste for politics, and little faith in the reasoning powers of the masses, especially of the peasants. Reason without ordered ideas is still far from being the force which lives in creative activity. There can be no ideas in the minds of the mass until the community of interests of all the separate individuals is realized.

When in 1917 Lenin on his arrival in Russia published his theses I thought that by these theses he was sacrificing to the Russian peasantry the small but heroic band of politically educated workers and all the genuine revolutionaries of the intelligentsia. The single active force in Russia, I thought, would be thrown like a handful of salt into the

Paris, 1912.

Sest

Petrograd, 1921.

Be

1914.

Petrograd, 1920.

1-22.

Berlin, 1922.

vapid bog of village life, and would dissolve without leaving any trace, would be sucked down without effecting any change in the mind, life, or history of the Russian people. The professional intelligentsia, in general, the scientists and technicians, were, from my point of view, revolutionaries by nature, and this socialist intelligentsia, together with the workers, were for me the most precious force stored up in Russia. In 1917 I did not see any other force capable of taking power, and organizing the village. But only on condition of complete inner unity could this force, numerically insignificant and split by contradictions, fulfill its role. Before them stood a tremendous task – to bring order into the anarchy of the village, to discipline the mind of the peasant, teach him to work rationally, to reorganize his economy, and by such means make the country progress. All this could only be achieved by subjecting the instincts of the village to the reason of the town.

The primary task of the revolution I considered to be the creation of the conditions which would lead to the development of the cultural forces of the country. To this end I offered to organize in Capri a school for workers, and in the years of reaction, from 1907 to 1913, I tried as much as I could to raise the spirits of the workers by every possible method.

In order to make myself quite clear I will add that all my life, the depressing effect of the prevalence of illiteracy in the village on the town, the individualism of the peasants, and their almost complete lack of social emotions had weighed heavily on my spirits. The dictatorship of the politically enlightened workers, in close connection with the scientific and technical intelligentsia, was, in my opinion, the only possible solution to a difficult situation which the war had made especially complicated by rendering the village still more anarchical. I differed from the Bolsheviks on the question of the value of the role of the intelligentsia in the Russian revolution, which had been prepared by this same intelligentsia, and to which had belonged all the Bolsheviks who had educated hundreds of workers in the spirit of social heroism and genuine intellectuality. The Russian intelligentsia, the scientific and professional intelligentsia, I thought, had always been, was still, and would long be the only beast of burden to drag along the heavy load of

Russian history. In spite of all shocks and impulses and stimulation which it had experienced, the mind of the masses of the people had remained a force still in need of leadership from without.

So I thought in 1917 – and was mistaken. . . . Of course, after a series of cases of the most despicable sabotage by a number of specialists, I had no alternative but to change my attitude toward the scientific and technical professionals. Such changes cost something – especially in old age.

I often used to speak with Lenin about the cruelty of revolutionary tactics and life.

"What do you want?" he would ask in astonishment and anger. "Is it possible to act humanely in a struggle of such unprecedented ferocity? Where is there any place for soft-heartedness or generosity? We are being blockaded by Europe, we are deprived of the help of the European proletariat, counter-revolution is creeping like a bear on us from every side. What do you want? Are we not right? Ought we not to struggle and resist? We are not a bunch of fools. We know that what we want can only be achieved by ourselves. . . ."

I often overwhelmed him with requests of a different nature, and often felt that all the bother I went to for various people made Lenin pity me. He would ask, "Don't you think you are wasting your energies on a lot of rubbish?"

But I continued to do what I thought ought to be done, and was not put off when the man who knew the enemies of the proletariat looked at me askance, in anger. He would shake his head crushingly and say, "You are compromising yourself in the eyes of the comrades and workers."

I pointed out that comrades and workers, when their passions were roused and they were irritated, not infrequently hold too lightly the life and liberty of valuable people, and that this in my view not only compromised the honest hard work of the revolution by too great, sometimes even senseless, cruelty, but was objectively and strategically bad, as it repelled many important people from participation in the revolution.

"H'm, h'm," Lenin muttered skeptically, and pointed out to me many cases when the intelligentsia betrayed the interests of the workers.

Yet I don't remember a single instance when any request

of mine met with a refusal from Ilyitch.

An old acquaintance of mine, P. A. Skorokhodov, another Sormovo worker, a tender-hearted man, complained of the painfulness of the work in the Cheka. I said to him, "I think that is not the right work for you. It isn't congenial to you." He agreed sadly, "Absolutely uncongenial." But after thinking a little, he said: "But you know Ilyitch too has to stifle his emotions, and I am ashamed to be so weak."

I knew and still know many workers who had to, and have to, grit their teeth hard, and stifle emotions, to overcome their organic "social idealism" for the sake of the triumph of the cause they are serving. Did Lenin too have to stifle his emotions?

"Our generation," [said Lenin] "achieved something of amazing significance for history. The cruelty, which the conditions of our life made necessary, will be understood and vindicated. Everything will be understood, everything." He caressed the children with great care, with an especially gentle and tender touch. *(Days with Lenin)*

However, Gorky continued to protest against the reign of terror, and in particular against the Soviet government's treatment of the intellectuals. He became a hindrance, and as he had suffered a relapse into illness, Lenin seized this pretext in order to get him out of Russia. In August, 1921, Gorky left for his second exile. He returned seven years later, in 1928, when the whole country celebrated his sixtieth birthday.

RETURN TO THE U.S.S.R.

Extracts from the speech delivered by Gorky at the plenary session of the Moscow Soviet, held in the Great Theater, in May, 1928, and dedicated to the writer's social, political, and literary activity; party and professional organization participating. (Transcript)

It can no longer be considered an exception that, after having overcome illiteracy and various other external obstacles, Alexei Peshkov became a man of letters relatively as able as those who have gone through the lycée and the university. This fact is not exceptional, for if, before his time, examples of this sort were rather few, today, among the 2500 builders of life and new culture present here, there are undoubtedly more than one hundred such cases. There must be thousands of biographies like mine in Russia.

I have become somewhat acquainted with these men, who inhabit the different corners of the Union. I know of ten or more whose lives were incomparably harder than mine. But comrades, let's abandon my biography, it is a story that is over and done with, and everyone has had enough of it. The question is not to know how man was, but how he is, today. And in general that has to do not with grandfathers or grandmothers, but little children. (Laughter. Applause.)

Seizing on the air of emotionalism, Gorky gave his listeners a lecture on friendship:

> Comrades, you must bring more kindness into your relationships, be less harsh. Each one of you is needed. Each one of you is a good worker. If not, you would have been unable to accomplish what you have. . . . You find it possible to be kind to me, then why should you be less so among yourselves? (Laughter.) That's not a funny question, it's quite serious. What does it mean that I have written twenty books? Literature is work like any other. Sure, it's good work, but the manufacture of surgical instruments is neither less good nor less difficult.
>
> That which you must and can create, ought to lead you to have a greater regard for one another. Appreciate each other, because you are worthy of being highly appreciated. Believe me, I am not exaggerating. I am not an artist telling you this, not a literary man, but a simple Russian worker. (Thunderous applause.) That is all, comrades. (Lively applause turning into an ovation; the orchestra plays the *Internationale.)*

Extracts from Gorky's speech at the plenary session of the Baku Soviet, in the summer of 1928:

> Comrades, today I have been called a happy man. That is correct; you see before you a genuinely happy man, a man whose greatest dreams, greatest hopes have come true. Perhaps the dreams were hazy, the hopes vague, but they kept me alive, gave a meaning to my life.
>
> If I were a critic and had to write on Maxim Gorky, I should say that the force which made him what he is, such as he is, here, before you, the writer that you love and appreciate so exaggeratedly, well, I should say that this force derives from his having been the first among Russian writers and perhaps the first in general to have understood directly and unaided, the tremendous value of work; work, creator of all that is beautiful, great, and precious in this world.
>
> They have said up here that nature accorded me certain gifts. I don't think so. I was born just like any one of you. Yes, that's what I think. And I know, too, that the nature whose beauty we admire and describe in word, color, music,

and in our culture, that nature was not part of my dreams. . . . I love it as you do, comrades, but there is another nature dearer to me, a nature which – let me express it by a word today in disgrace – a nature which I respect and venerate as holy. It is the nature issuing from the hands of men, the second nature that we on earth create, in standing up to the first.

I do not know how, but it happens, comrades, that I learned that very early, without the help of books. Until I was twenty-three, twenty-four or twenty-five, I shared the life of labor of all the working people of my time, my generation. I had to bear what you yourselves bore, I had to combat the same parasites, the same hunger, the same cold. . . . I understood it before I got to know Marx's doctrine. As a rule, men understand these things before taking up Marx or similar writings. They understand them intuitively. That's what happened to me.

Comrades, what man does is more important than what nature does. . . . Nature confines itself to giving us life, it is up to us to do the rest. . . . It is we who are the creators of the second nature.

So, comrades, it is without importance that, for certain reasons, Alexei Peshkov has become Maxim Gorky. What is important, comrades, is man's will reaching out towards a goal.

What is important is to be the man one wants to be and to accomplish freely that which man wishes. Conditions are with us today.

Gorky was overwhelmed by the results obtained in ten years of work. Long before, following a meeting in the early days of the revolution, he had heard a soldier declare in a tone of complete certainty:

"We will take the earth into our hands, absolutely! And we will rebuild everything."

"The earth, will you make it round like a watermelon?" was the sarcastic question from a gentleman in a visored cap.

"Yes!" confirmed the soldier.

"Will you raze the mountains?"

"And why not, if they are in the way?"

"And shall the rivers run up-stream?"

"They will flow where we make them flow. Why are you laughing, *barin*?" *(Through the Soviet Union,* 1929)

A new type of man is springing up in the Soviet Union, and his characteristics may already be defined without fear of error.

He possesses a faith in the organizing power of reason, a faith that has been lost by the European intellectuals, who have been exhausted by the sterile labor of reconciling class contradictions. He is conscious of being the builder of a new world, and although his conditions of life are still arduous, he knows that it is his aim and the purposes of his rational will to create different conditions – and he has no grounds for pessimism. He is young historically as well as biologically. *(The Old Man and the New)*

My joy and my pride is the new Russian man, the builder of the new state.

To this small, but great man, who is to be found in all the remotest and wildest parts of the country, in factories and villages, and cast away in the steppe and the Siberian forests, in the Caucasian mountains and in the Northern tundra; to the man who is sometimes very lonely, working among people who still find it hard to understand him; to the servant of his state, who is modestly performing a job that seems to be insignificant, but whose historical significance is tremendous – to him, I address my sincere greetings. Comrade, be steadfast in the knowledge that you are the most necessary man on earth! In doing your small job, you have really begun to create a new world. (*Ten Years,* 1927)

THE MASTER

There are few famous writers to whom the name of "master" – guide and support of the young – is better suited than to Gorky.

Every time the postman brings me a gray notebook of inexpensive paper, covered with a clumsy script and accompanied by a letter in which an unknown but familiar person, invisible yet near, asks me to "leaf through" his literary attempts and tell him "if he has talent, if he is worthy of attention," my heart contracts with joy and pain and lights up with a great hope and renewed suspense.

My joy comes from the fact that, more and more often, I am sent these awkward verses, this unskilled prose, and the voices of those who write ring louder and stronger. One senses that in the lower strata men are becoming more aware of their ties with the world, and that, small, they aspire ever more fervently to a great and expanded life and to freedom. With what fervor they seek to communicate their new thoughts, to encourage their weary fellow creatures, and to appreciate this poor world!

And what enthusiastic power in the hope that soon our oppressed people will hold their heads high and will rise up;

> and that, awakened, animated with new strength, they will assume their share in the creation of a new culture, and a new history.
>
> We have before us a tremendous task of rebuilding Russia on new foundations. We need to see to it that the forces of culture develop and accumulate. We possess pitifully little in the way of the needs of today and our difficult tomorrow.
>
> And yet, nowhere is man so under-valued as here, and nowhere is he as impotent. . . . We live among a very talented people, the proof being that no western country produces such a high percentage of self-educated people: writers, technicians, founders of sects. Now, if that has been possible under such difficult, such abominable conditions, we are right in having confidence in the gifts and the spiritual strength of our people. (Preface to the book by the peasant, Ivan Morozov, *The Enchanted Grass.)*

Swamped by letters from beginners asking his advice, Gorky answered them in his pamphlet, *How I Became a Writer* (1928), in which he summed up his career as a writer, analyzing it in the terms used by his correspondents, self-educated writers. Some declared they wrote to escape from a monotonous life and others declared that they sought to unburden themselves in writing.

> When I was about twenty years old I began to understand that I had seen, heard, and experienced many things about which I ought to and indeed must tell other people. It seemed to me that I understood and felt certain things in a different way from other people. This worried me and made me restless and talkative. Even when reading such a master as Turgenev, I sometimes thought that perhaps I might tell the stories of the heroes in *A Sportsman's Sketches* in a different way from Turgenev. At this time I was already regarded as an interesting story-teller, and dockers, bakers, tramps, carpenters, railway-workers, "pilgrims to holy places," and in general people among whom I was living would listen to me with attention. When I told them about books I had read I caught myself more and more often telling the stories differently, distorting what I had read, adding something to it out of my own experience. This happened because for me literature and life had merged into one; a book was

the same sort of manifestation of life as a man, a book was also a living, speaking reality, and it was less a "thing" than were all other things created or to be created by man.

Intellectuals who listened to me told me:

"Write! Try to write!"

Often I felt as if drunk and was subject to fits of loquacity, a sort of wordy debauch resulting from my desire to speak of everything that grieved or gladdened me; I wanted to relieve myself by speaking of it. I had moments of tormenting tension when I had a lump in my throat like an hysterical woman. I wanted to shout aloud that Anatoli the glazier, my friend and a very gifted lad, would perish if no one helped him; that Theresa, the streetwalker, was a good woman and that it was an injustice that she was a prostitute and that the students who used her did not understand this just as they did not understand that Matitsa, the old beggar woman, was more intelligent than Yakovleva, our bookish young midwife.

Without telling even my close friend, the student Guri Pletnev, I wrote some verses about Theresa and Anatoli, about the snow which melted in spring but did not do so in order to drip down in a stream of dirty water from the street into the cellar where the bakers were working; I wrote that the Volga was a beautiful river, that the pretzel-maker Kuzin was Judas Iscariot, and that life was a swinish and painful business that killed the soul.

Writing verses came easily to me but I saw that my verses were vile and I despised myself for my lack of skill and talent. I read Pushkin, Lermontov, Nekrasov, Kurochin's translations of Béranger, and saw perfectly well that I was not in the least like any of these poets. I was afraid to write prose because it seemed to me that prose was much more difficult than verse; prose demanded especially sharp eyes, the ability to see and observe things invisible to others, and a certain exceptionally compact and powerful arrangement of words. But for all that I did try to write prose as well, preferring, however, to write rhythmical prose, because I found the writing of ordinary prose beyond my powers. The results of these attempts of mine were simply pitiful and ridiculous. I wrote an enormously long poem in rhythmical prose which I called "Song of the Old Oak." In ten words V. G. Korolenko demolished this "wooden" production. . .

But that didn't cure me of my passion for the form and five years later, Korolenko, while praising my story *Grandfather Arkhip*, declared that I was wrong to pepper it with something that "resembled poetry." I didn't believe him, but at home, on rereading the story, I had to admit with despair that one entire page – the description of a downpour on the steppe – had been written in that blasted "rhythm." For a long time it pursued me, working its way into all my stories, imperceptibly and inappropriately. They all began with melodious sentences. . . . In general, I had a compulsion to "prettify."

"The sea laughed," I wrote, and for a long time I thought it was good. Enamored of beauty, I committed sin after sin against the precision of descriptions, I placed objects badly, I illumined people all wrong. L. N. Tolstoy made this observation concerning my story *Twenty-six and One*: "Your stove is in the wrong place." And in fact, the flames from the oven could not have shone on the workmen the way I wrote it. Concerning Medinskaia, in *Foma Gordeiev,* A. P. Chekhov said:

"But, my dear fellow, she has three ears, one of which is on her chin, see for yourself!" It was so: I had painted her most unfortunately.

I do not consider myself a master capable of creating characters and types equalling in artistic merit such types and characters as Oblomov, Rudin, Bazarov, etc. But even in order to write *Foma Gordeiev* I had to observe many a dozen merchants' sons who were dissatisfied with their fathers' lives and professions. They all had a vague feeling that there was little point in their monotonous, "poor and wearisome" life. The prototypes of my Foma, doomed to a dull life, resenting it, and given to brooding, either took to drink and became debauchées, men who "burned up life," or else they became such "white ravens" as Sava Morozov [the fabulously wealthy industrialist], who paid the expenses of Lenin's *Iskra*, or M. A. Machkov, the owner of river transports in Perm, who subsidized the Social Revolutionary party.

Young people have asked my why I wrote about tramps.

Because living among the lower middle class and seeing around me people whose only object was to exploit other people by hook or crook, to turn other people's blood and

Russia, 1917. A group of workers getting rifle practice.

sweat into kopeks and turn the kopeks into rubles, I, like my fifteen-year-old correspondent, came to hate fiercely the parasitic life of these commonplace people who resembled each other like copper coins from the same mint.

Tramps for me were "uncommon" people, they were uncommon because they were "declassed," men who had cut loose from their class or had been repudiated by it and had lost the most characteristic traits of their class. . . . Most of these people were diseased and drunkards; fights between them were frequent, but ties of comradely mutual assistance were well developed among them and everything that they managed to earn or steal they ate and drank in common.

A brawl among some tramps in front of the night shelter in Nizhni Novgorod. Inscriptions on the building: "No singing," "No noise-making."

I saw that although their living conditions were worse than those of ordinary people, they considered themselves better and indeed they felt better than ordinary people because they were not greedy, they did not try to get the better of each other, they did not hoard money. . . .

There were strange people among these tramps and there were a lot of things about them I did not understand, but I was greatly biased in their favor by the fact that they did not complain of life and spoke of the comfortable life of the respectable people sarcastically or ironically yet not out of a feeling of concealed envy, not because the grapes were sour, but rather out of a feeling of pride, out of the knowledge that although they were "living badly," they were nevertheless better men than those who were "living well."

So I would say that my prediliction for tramps resulted from my desire to portray "uncommon" people rather than the mean petty-bourgeois types. Of course, this was partly due to the influence of foreign, and especially French, literature, much brighter and more colorful than our Russian. But what moved me above all was the desire to embellish with my own imagination the "beggarly, wearisome life" about which my fifteen-year-old girl correspondent wrote.

This desire, as I have already said, is called "romanticism." Certain critics have tried to see in my romanticism a reflection of philosophical idealism. I don't think so.

For me, there are no ideas beyond man; for me, man and only man is the creator of all things and all ideas, he is the miracle-worker and the future master of all the forces of nature. The most beautiful things in this our world are the things made by labor, made by skilled human hands, and all our thoughts, all our ideas, are born out of the process of labor, as shown by the whole history of the arts, science, and technology. Thoughts come after the facts. I bow to man because beyond the incarnations of man's reason and imagination, I feel and see nothing in our world. God has been one of man's inventions, just like photography, with the difference that the latter fixes that which really exists, whereas God is a photo of an idea which man invents, of a being who wishes – and is able – to be omniscient, omnipotent, and perfectly just.

And if it is thought necessary to speak of sacred things, then the one sacred thing is the dissatisfaction of man with himself and his striving to be better than he is; sacred is his hatred of all the trivial rubbish which he himself has created; sacred is his desire to do away with greed, envy, crime, disease, war, and all enmity between men on earth; and sacred is his labor.

Chronology

1861 Abolition of serfdom.

1868 March 16 (28): birth of Alexei Maximovitch Peshkov, at Nizhni Novgorod on the Volga. Son of Maxim Peshkov, carpenter, and Varvara, daughter of Kashirin the dyemaker. Tolstoy was forty years old. He published *War and Peace* (1864-69). Dostoevsky was forty-seven. Condemned in 1849 to Siberian imprisonment following a political conspiracy, he had been back since 1859, politically and religiously repentant. Chekhov was eight, and Korolenko, five.

1870 Birth of Lenin at Simbirsk on the Volga.

1878 Trepov, governor of Petersburg, having caused a political prisoner to be whipped, was shot by Vera Zasulitch. The affair brought about great agitation of opinion in her favor. Her trial became a milestone in the history of the revolutionary movement. She was acquitted.

1880 Publication of *The Brothers Karamazov*. Tolstoy's moral crisis and beginnings of Tolstoyism: the preaching of non-resistance to evil.

1881 On the occasion of the unveiling of the Pushkin monument in Moscow, Dostoevsky delivered his famous speech calling the Russians to resignation. He died the same year. Assassination of Alexander II by a group of revolutionaries. Accession of Alexander III. Reaction became more pronounced. Execution of Alexander Ulianov, Lenin's older brother, following an attempt against Alexander III.

1888 Attempt against the Imperial family in Borki.

October Street in Gorky
(formerly Nizhni Novgorod).

1894 Death of Alexander III. Accession of Nicholas II.

1895 Lenin brought about the union of socialist and workers' groups, beginning new phase in history of Russian revolution.

1897 Lenin deported to Siberia for three years. Founding of Moscow Art Theater by Stanislavsky and Nemirovitch-Danchenko.

1904-05 Death of Chekhov. The war with Japan ended in disaster for Russia. Series of terrorist acts perpetrated by revolutionaries.

1905 January 9 (22): 'Bloody Sunday': workers, gathered before Winter Palace under Father Gapon's leadership, met with brutal rifle-fire. October 17: first Russian revolution. The Czar, under pressure, granted constitution and parliament – Duma.

1910 Death of Tolstoy.

1917 February 27 (March 11): February Revolution. October 25 (November 7): October Revolution.

1935 Romain Rolland in Soviet Union.

1936 June 18: Death of Gorky following seige of pneumonia. Last guard of honor taken by Stalin, Molotov, Kaganovitch, Ordzhonikidze, Andreyev, Mikoyan, Zhdanov. National mourning. Urn containing Gorky's ashes sealed into Kremlin wall, alongside Red Square.

With Romain Rolland, near Moscow.

L. to r., Molotov, Ordzhonikidze, Stalin and Kaganovitch bearing Gorky's ashes.

Bibliography

Articles and Pamphlets (Foreign Languages Publishing House, Moscow 1951).

Autobiography of Maxim Gorky: My Childhood, In the World, My Universities (New York, The Citadel Press, 1949).

Best Short Stories of Maxim Gorky, edited by Yarmolinsky and Budberg (New York, Grayson Publishing Corp., 1947).

The Confession (New York, Frederick A. Stokes Company, 1916).

Culture and the People (New York, International Publishers, 1939).

Days with Lenin (New York, International Publishers, 1932).

Foma Gordeiev (New York, Charles Scribner's Sons, 1901).

Fragments from My Diary (London, Philip Allan & Co., 1924).

Letters of Gorky and Andreyev, 1899-1912 (New York, Columbia University Press, 1958).

Literary Portraits (Moscow, Foreign Languages Publishing House).

Literature and Life (London, Hutchinson International Authors, Ltd., 1946).

Mother (New York, D. Appleton and Company, 1923).

On Guard for the Soviet Union (London, Martin Lawrence, 1933).

Orloff and His Wife: Tales of the Barefoot Brigade (New York, Charles Scribner's Sons, 1906).

Orphan Paul (New York, Boni and Gaer, 1946). (Contains the essay, *How I Became a Writer.*)

Problems of Soviet Literature (New York, International Publishers, 1935).

Reminiscences of Leo Nikolaevich Tolstoy (New York, B. W. Huebsch, Inc., 1920).

Selected Short Stories (Moscow, Foreign Languages Publishing House).

Seven Plays (New Haven, Yale University Press, 1945).

Through Russia (New York, E. P. Dutton & Co.).

Twenty-six and One and Other Stories (New York, Brentano's, 1906).

Unrequited Love (London, George Weidenfeld & Nicolson Limited, 1949).

Suggested readings by other authors:

To the Finland Station, Edmund Wilson (Garden City, Doubleday and Company, Inc., 1940).

A History of Russian Literature, D. S. Mirsky (New York, Alfred A. Knopf, 1949).

The Letters of Lenin (New York, Harcourt, Brace and Company, 1937).

Maxim Gorky and His Russia, Alexander Kaun (New York, Jonathan Cape and Harrison Smith, 1931).

Acknowledgments

Some of the documents reproduced in this book come from the *Complete Soviet Encyclopedia* and the new edition of Gorky's *Complete Works.* The others were furnished by the print room of the *Bibliothèque Nationale, L'Institut d'Études Slaves, l'École Nationale des Langues Orientales,* and the *Cinémathèque Française.* The plates on page 181 and on the inside front cover are *Roger Viollet* pictures. Acknowledgement is made to the following publishers for permission to quote brief passages: Columbia University Press, *The Young Maxim Gorky,* by Filia Holtzman; International Publishers, *Culture and the People,* by Maxim Gorky; Citadel Press, *The Mother,* by Maxim Gorky.